FAITH & FAMILY

HAROLD S. KUSHNER

FAITH & FAMILY

Favorite Sermons of Rabbi Harold S. Kushner

Franz Rosenzweig Comes Home and *The First Question* originally appeared in *Commanded to Live*, published by Hartmore House/Media Judaica and reprinted by permission.

ISBN 978-0-9798843-0-6
PRINTED IN CHINA

COVER & BOOK DESIGN: Debra M Beck • Studio18Group.com
AUTHOR PHOTO BY: Suzette Kushner

This book was set in Sabon.

ALSO BY RABBI HAROLD S. KUSHNER

Commanded to Live

When Children Ask About God

When Bad Things Happen to Good People

When All You've Ever Wanted Isn't Enough

Who Needs God

To Life!

How Good Do We Have to Be?

Living a Life That Matters

The Lord Is My Shepherd

Overcoming Life's Disappointments

CONTENTS

FORWARD

Spoken words are such insubstantial things. They float in the air for a second or two and then they vanish. Yet we all know, and religion endorses the notion, that words are as real as any physical object. The right words can heal and comfort; the wrong words can hurt and alienate.

Sermons, composed of words, are intellectual mayflies, here for a moment and then gone. They take hours to craft and only a few minutes to deliver. At best, they are heard only by those present at a given service. In reality, some of those present may not even be listening. Others will hear the sermon and misunderstand it, and still others will hear it and forget it. And once or twice a year, someone will come up to me and tell me that something I said in a sermon years ago changed his or her life.

For all of those reasons, I was deeply gratified when the leadership of my congregation, Temple Israel of Natick, Massachusetts, where I was the rabbi for many years and where I am now a member with the title of Rabbi Laureate, asked me to assemble eighteen of my favorite sermons for publication in this volume.

As you will see, several themes persist throughout the book:

- the notion that religion cannot protect us from misfortune but can give us the resources to cope with it;

- the insistence that the human soul is fashioned in the image of God, unique in its ability to distinguish between good and evil and in its ability to conjure up such divine qualities as generosity, forgiveness and love;

- the confidence that, no matter how much things change in the world around us, the wisdom of the past is a reliable guide to help us meet the challenges of the present;

- and the importance of community, people coming together to sustain each other and to help each other find things none of us could find on our own.

I am grateful to Steven Karas and Lynne Satlof-Karas for spearheading this effort, to Sue Rodgin for transcribing some decades-old manuscripts, to graphic designer Debra Beck for preparing the sermons for publication, and most of all to my wife Suzette for knowing even before I did how much the publication of this volume would mean to me.

And a final word of thanks to the members of Temple Israel of Natick for sharing with me their fears, their concerns, their hopes and their questions, and for listening while I tried to answer them.

Rabbi Harold S. Kushner
Natick, Massachusetts
October 2007

FAITH

IF I COULD CHANGE ONE THING
about the world for this coming year,
that would be it – that every human being
come to recognize that certain things
are wrong and should not be done, that
hurting people is wrong, that cheating
people is wrong, that a religion that
endorses, even celebrates the murder of
innocent people is a false religion.

A Prayer for the New Year

Rosh HaShanah 2003

To gather on the first day of a New Year is inevitably to stand at the intersection of the emotions of fear and hope, to be painfully aware of all the bad things that might happen to our families, to our world, and at the same time to cling to the dreams of what a blessed future might hold for us. We read the headlines about war and terrorism and killing, but as we open a new calendar, we once again hope that this will be the year when the human race finally gets it right and learns to live as God intended us to live.

As always at the most anxious times of our lives, we turn to the prayerbook to give us the words to express the deepest longings of our hearts. And what does the prayerbook say to us this morning? What would it have us pray for, to bring peace and healing to a broken and bloodstained world?

People who are unfamiliar with Jewish prayer think we spend all these hours in synagogue on Rosh HaShanah asking God for things, begging God for things, because that is what they think prayer is, and they are not entirely comfortable with that because it has never worked for them before. When they were young, they might have prayed for a bicycle but they didn't get a bicycle, or if they did, they had reason to believe it wasn't God who gave it to them. They might have prayed for a boy friend or a girl friend and ended up questioning not God's power but God's taste. When they were older, they might have prayed for a favorable report from their doctor, and sometimes they got it and sometimes they didn't, but they had trouble seeing where prayer affected the outcome.

But that's really not what Jewish prayer is about. Jewish prayer is not about asking, not about begging. A non-Jewish friend once asked me "What do Jews pray for?" and I told her "Jews don't really pray <u>for</u>, so much as they pray <u>to</u> and they pray <u>with</u>." Most of the prayers we recite this morning aren't meant for God's ears; they are meant for us. They come to remind us to be grateful. They come to teach us how to recognize God's presence in our lives. The prayer Netaneh Tokef, the emotional centerpiece of the Rosh HaShanah liturgy, the one that speaks of it being "decided on Rosh HaShanah and confirmed on Yom Kippur who shall live and who shall die," is not a prayer to God to inscribe us in the Book of Life. It's a lesson for us, to teach us that some of the things that will happen to us in the coming year are beyond our control, but that prayer, charity and a change of values can make those bad things hurt less. To the man who is diagnosed with a serious illness and complains to me "So what good did all that going to shul on Shabbos do me?", the answer is "It should have given you the resources to cope with this turn of events and not be totally shattered by it."

Jewish prayer is studying, pausing in our service to hear words of Torah. And Jewish prayer is congregating, coming together to rediscover the great truth that the same words come out different when you say them together with others in the setting of a congregation.

But there is one point in the service where we do ask for something, where we do ask God to make things different in the New Year, and it's not for ourselves. We ask God to make the world different in three ways. It comes in the middle of the first and second recitations of the Amidah, the place where prayers of petition are traditionally inserted. Listen closely to what we ask for: how would we like the world to be different next year from the kind of world it was in the year just ended?

Our first request: *Uv'chen ten pach'decha al kol ma'asecha v'yirat'cha al kol mah she-baratta.* May all of God's creatures come to know the fear of God. Now you have to understand that, in the Bible, the phrase "the fear of God" has nothing to do with being afraid. It doesn't refer to fear of being punished or fear of going to hell when you die. "The fear of God" means a sense of morality, an awareness that certain things are wrong and should not be done. At the beginning of the book of Exodus, when Pharaoh decrees that all male Israelite babies should be killed, we read that "the Egyptian midwives feared God" and disobeyed Pharaoh's orders. That is, they refused to do it because they knew it was wrong.

If I could change one thing about the world for this coming year, that would be it – that every human being come to recognize that certain things are wrong and should not be done, that hurting people is wrong, that cheating people is wrong, that a religion that endorses, even celebrates, the murder of innocent people is a false religion, that your sense of grievance against society for the way your life turned out does not give you license to strike out in blind rage against that society, whether you are an inner city teenager, a man who's just been fired from his factory job, or an unemployed Palestinian. Some things are simply wrong, not just illegal, not just a matter of "what kind of world would it be if everybody did that?", but wrong. That's what made our first ancestors, Adam and Eve, different from the animals. They acquired a knowledge of good and evil.

Why is that so hard to understand? Why is it that, when Baruch Goldstein snapped under the strain of seeing his friends murdered, took a gun and killed two dozen innocent Muslims at prayer, virtually every Rabbi in America and in Israel condemned what he did as a desecration of Jewish values, but when Palestinian suicide bombers blow up a crowded bus or restaurant, we are asked to understand that this was an understandable response to what they had gone through.

One reason is that popular culture, pop psychology and movies have taught us that feelings are more important than anything else.

Feelings are self-justifying. "Why did you do it?" "Because I was angry." And that's meant, not as an explanation but as a justification. The psychological insight that people are not responsible for their feelings and should not feel guilty for their thoughts has somehow been distorted into the notion that people are not responsible for what they do based on those feelings.

Sometimes a person with a conscience will say "I'm not happy doing this but it will lead to a greater good, so I'll give myself permission," which is why the word "rationalize" exists in the English language. "Rationalize" means persuading yourself that something is all right when you really know that it isn't. So you get politicians lying to get what they want. You get church leaders covering up serious crimes to protect the institution rather than to protect its most vulnerable members. The scandal of the Roman Catholic Church is not that fewer than one percent of its priests did something detestable. That can happen in any population. The scandal is that prominent religious leaders, when they learned of it, were incapable of calling it wrong.

Would you like to be able to get on an airplane this coming year without having to worry that something might happen, without having to remove your wallet, your shoes, your belt buckle to prove you're not a terrorist? Would you like to pick up your morning paper and not be shocked or dismayed by what you read? Would you like to spend less of your money on security systems, burglar alarms? Read the real estate ads for expensive apartments in New York City. They are not about location. They are all about security: doorman, 24-hour-concierge, one-entrance building, or in Florida, gated community. Would you like to get away from all that? This would be the place to start, our first and chief wish for the New Year: May all of God's creatures come to understand that some things, no matter how tempting or emotionally satisfying they may be, are wrong and should not be done.

Do I get a second wish? My second wish would be the second paragraph of the Rosh HaShanah liturgy of the Amidah: *uv'chen ten kavod l'amecha, simcha l'artzecha v'sasson l'irecha.* May God grant honor to His people, happiness to His land and joy to His city of Jerusalem. My second wish is that Israel be treated more fairly in the press than it generally is. I have been outraged and sickened by the way Israel has been portrayed in the media, by the policies of so many European governments, and by the utterly shameful behavior of the United Nations. I don't believe the situation in the Middle East justifies a balanced approach, equal time for each side's point of view. I may consider all violence distasteful and unfortunate, but I will insist that there is a distinction between the violence of the bank robber and the violence of the bank guard in resisting him. There is a moral difference between killing a mass murderer who is resisting arrest, and killing two-dozen young people in a coffee house.

But at this point I would settle for evenhandedness in place of the malicious, distorted Israel-bashing that we so often find in the press. I believe that the American Jewish community has been betrayed by the American left, by the progressive movement in this country to which so many American Jews have been devoted for so long. It calls to mind a passage in the Hebrew epic poem MASSADA, where a group of young idealists come together to try to make this a better world. One of them, the only Jewish member of the group, takes off his shirt and makes it into a banner on which he writes "All men are brothers." The others then take his banner and march off with it, leaving him behind half-naked.

The left in this country permitted the protests against the invasion of Iraq to be hijacked and turned into rallies for the Palestinians. They permitted themselves to be talked into seeing the Palestinians as victims rather than those who have prevented peace for the past half-century or more. And the sad part of it, above and beyond the unjustified defamation of Israel, is that Jews may be alienated from such liberal causes as racial and economic justice because the people advocating them most prominently are also among the shrillest advocates of the Palestinian cause.

Last June, the Unitarian Church held their national convention here in Boston and they invited me to speak. One of the things I said to them was "I know that the Unitarian Universalist Association has a standing committee on the rights of the Palestinians. I would be pleasantly surprised to be told that you also have a standing committee on the security and survival of Israel, and if you don't, you might want to ask yourselves why not? Why wouldn't you want to support the only country in that part of the world that has a free press and guarantees the rights of women and gays?"

Last year was the centennial of the birth of George Orwell, and there were many times last year when I found myself thinking of Orwell and his novel 1984. If you remember, Orwell's hero, Winston Smith, works for a government agency called the Ministry of Truth, where his job is to rewrite the encyclopedias and history books to make the past reflect the claims and policies of the current government. When the book was written a half-century ago, that sounded like somebody's futuristic nightmare, but there are a lot of places in the world today where that is precisely what is happening. Not everyone has the same definition of Truth that we do, - an accurate, unbiased account of what really happened. For a lot of people in a lot of places, Truth is whatever supports and endorses their view of the world. If you find that idea hard to get your head around, think of a parent who convinces herself that the teacher is unfairly prejudiced against her son because she can't handle the idea that her son is a mediocre student. So when Saudi and Egyptian intellectuals, educated people, can believe that the attack on the World Trade Center was a Zionist plot, when Yasser Arafat says that there was never a Temple in Jerusalem and his spokesman refers to the Israeli control of the West Bank as "the most brutal occupation in history," even though anyone who has taken a college course in world history could list fifty cases that were immeasurably worse, from the Spanish in South America to the Chinese in Tibet - I don't think that they see themselves as lying. They believe that what they are saying is true, not factually true, not because that is what really happened, but true in the sense that it reinforces what they need to believe about the world.

And that's fine with me if that's what they want to do. If some individual chooses to avoid doctors and depend on prayer to heal him, if somebody wants to jump out of the window because he doesn't believe in the law of gravity, that's his problem. It becomes our problem when Western media feel they have to give equal time and plausibility to those hallucinatory statements.

I hope that everyone in this congregation who cares about Israel will do what my wife and I have learned to do, and that is to turn a deaf ear to the incessant fund-raising appeals on National Public Radio because of their undeniably anti-Israel, pro-Palestinian slanting of the news, which they don't even have the integrity to admit to. I'm sorry I have to say this, because they do so many things well. But I don't want my money going to promote sympathy for Palestinian terrorists and for an inaccurate, distorted image of Israel.

That is not censorship. If someone chooses not to buy my books because he doesn't like what I write, he is not censoring my writings. And if I choose not to support an organization because I disapprove of its policies on a matter that means a lot to me, that is not censorship either.

UV'chen ten kavod l'amecha. May Your people be treated honorably in the coming year. May all the world come to see Israel as we see it, a heroic, beleaguered people yearning for peace but compelled by its enemies to spend its resources on defense rather than on sustaining the poor, the immigrant, the left-behind. Israel may not be a perfect society, but it is an honorable one, at least as much as our country is. And Judaism is an honorable religion. And it is simply wrong for the Jewish people and the Jewish state to be the victims of defamation as we were in the year just ended. May the New Year see that change.

There is one more line in the prayer we have been discussing, virtually the only asking prayer in the whole lengthy Rosh HaShanah service. It reads:

Uv'chen tzaddikim yir'u v'yismachu v'hassidim y'ranenu. In this coming year, may the righteous have reason to rejoice and the pious have cause for happiness. Or as I would paraphrase it, may this world become a world in which good people will feel at home, a world that will give them, and will give God, reasons to say "this is my kind of place."

Last month, I was invited to speak at the memorial service for a young teenage girl from the western part of the state who was abducted and killed three years ago and whose remains were only recently found. Speaking to her grieving family and her angry and confused high school classmates, I asked what her death might teach us about the kind of world we live in. I suggested, "On one side of the scale, we have one evil person who did this terrible thing. On the other side, we have the hundreds of people, friends, neighbors and total strangers, who volunteered for a search party, the thousands who wrote letters and included the girl's family in their prayers, the many hundreds who turned out for her memorial service. One man devoted to cruelty and thousands dedicated to kindness. I can live in a world like that."

I still believe that. But I also have to acknowledge that all the kindness and all the comfort and all the prayers of those thousands of people never really balance out the terrible void left by that one person's cruelty. It helps but it doesn't really make up for it. It won't ever really be the world we yearn for, it won't really ever be the world God yearns for, until the cruelty disappears entirely and the world becomes a world full of kind people. If that is really our wish, if that is really our prayer for the New Year, maybe the place to start is to stop admiring toughness, to stop rewarding ruthlessness in business and in politics, and to educate for kindness as the chief currency of success.

Standing as we are at the intersection of hope and fear, buffeted on one side by predictions of what might happen, graced on the other side by the prayerbook's vision of a possible world, we pray: We pray that God open the eyes of every living man and woman to the truth that some things are wrong and should not be done.

We pray that God's promise to Abraham be fulfilled, that all nations of the world come to realize how much they are blessed by the children of Abraham, by the faith of Abraham, and by the land God promised to Abraham.

We pray that this coming year will give good people everywhere reasons to rejoice, that the world will echo with the laughter of children, the rejoicing of happy families and the benediction of the Creator of the world who will look down on His creation, and in the words of the old Jewish lady speaking to God on Rosh HaShanah, "God, this year may you have nachas from Your children."

I BELIEVE THE TEST

was to see whether Abraham's conscience

had matured to the point where it could

distinguish between the authentic

and the inauthentic voice of God.

Beyond Obedience

Rosh HaShanah 2005

This morning marks the fortieth time it has been my privilege to officiate at High Holy Day services here at Temple Israel. In all those years, I don't think I have ever given a really satisfying sermon based on the story we read from the Torah today and every year on Rosh HaShanah, the story of God commanding Abraham to offer up his son Isaac as a sacrifice. It is a troubling story. It has always troubled me, as I would hope it has troubled you. After many years of frustration, a child is born to Abraham and Sarah. They are overjoyed, not only for their personal fulfillment but also because it assures them that their distinctive way of life will be continued beyond their time. Then as the child begins to grow up, God commands Abraham to take his son to the mountaintop and offer him as a sacrifice, as apparently many religions of that time required of their believers. Abraham is ready to do God's bidding, but at the last moment, God intervenes and tells him he doesn't have to do it after all. A ram is substituted on the altar, and father and son go home together.

I have never been comfortable with that story. I don't know who bothers me more, God for making that demand, toying with the emotions of His most devoted follower, or Abraham for so readily agreeing to go along with God's demand. It's hard to think well of either of them. As I studied the commentaries and explanations scholars and apologists have given, I was horrified by what it drove thoughtful religious people to say, justifying what God did, praising Abraham for his obedience, warning us never to question

God, urging us to suspend our sense of the ethical in the face of God's demands.

There was a movie some years ago called "The Immigrants," about a farming community in Sweden whose inhabitants came to America together and settled in the Upper Midwest. One of the immigrants was the pastor of their church. In the course of their crossing the Atlantic, the pastor's child becomes ill and dies. They have a funeral service on board ship before they bury him at sea. In his eulogy, the pastor says, "God commanded us not to worship idols. I turned my son into an idol. I loved him more than I loved God, and so God has taken him from me to remove the source of my sin." And I remember sitting there in the theatre and saying to myself, "That's sick. Why would anyone in his right mind worship a God like that? Why would anyone belong to a religion like that?"

So there I was, year after year confronted by this baffling story and totally unable to make sense of it. Then one day this past year, I read an essay that pointed out a detail I had missed in the dozens of times I had read the story. Professor Marsha Mirkin of Brandeis University wrote a book called *The Women Who Danced by the Sea*. In it, she has a chapter on the Abraham-and-Isaac story in which she points out that, as the father and son are walking up the mountain, the presumption is that, when they get to the top, they will sacrifice a lamb. That's what people in those days generally did. Isaac says to his father, *Hineh ha-esh v'ha-etzim v'ayeh haseh l'olah*, We have the wood, we have the fire-starter, but where is the lamb we're going to sacrifice? Abraham answers him, *Elohim yir'eh lo haseh b'ni*, God will provide the lamb, my son (or, if you will, God will provide the lamb, namely my son). At that point Isaac begins to intuit that *he* is going to be the sacrificial lamb.

But then, at the climactic moment of the story – and this is the detail I kept missing all those years – God *doesn't* provide a lamb. God provides a *full-grown sheep. V'hineh ayil achar ne-ehaz bis'vach.* There was a *ram* caught in the thicket. What is a ram? A ram is a lamb's father.

Now, if the lamb would have represented a substitute for Isaac being sacrificed, what does the ram, the full-grown adult sheep, represent? It represents Abraham sacrificing a part of himself instead of sacrificing his son. And what part of himself? I would like to think that he is asked to *give up* his understanding of religion as unquestioning obedience.

I picture God saying to him, "Abraham, what on earth did you think you were doing? How could you possibly have believed that killing your child was the will of God? Did it never occur to you that I stand for life and not for death, for kindness and not cruelty? Have you completely forgotten that I gave you a conscience, that I planted in you the ability to distinguish between right and wrong, between good and bad, between that which a person should do and that which a person should never do? Have you forgotten that you are a descendant of Adam and Eve who ate the fruit of the Knowledge of Good and Evil, and learned in a way that no animal could understand that some things are not to be done? You were about to kill the child and blame Me for it, weren't you?"

Why are we so eager to define piety as unquestioning obedience to what represents itself as the word of God? Shouldn't we, of all people, have learned by now that "I was only following orders" is not exactly the hallmark of a religious person, a person to be admired? Why do we continue to defend that mentality?

For one thing, in a confusing world like the one we live in, there is something seductive about having someone tell you what to do. I think that is one of the reasons behind the unanticipated resurgence of fundamentalism across so many societies today. As life becomes more and more complicated, as we are confronted with issues about life and death, war and peace, human cloning, issues of business ethics and sexual behavior, we would love to have someone tell us what to do and think, and spare us the discomfort of having to decide.

Early in his novel *The Brothers Karamazov*, Dostoevsky gives us the parable of the Grand Inquisitor. He imagines Jesus coming back to earth in 15th Century Spain at the height of the Inquisition. He begins working miracles, reviving the dead, opening the eyes of the blind. Adoring crowds recognize him and gather around him. At that point, the Cardinal of Seville, the Grand Inquisitor, has him arrested and tells him that the next day, he will be burned at the stake as a heretic. Why? The cardinal explains that he is offering the people freedom and people don't really want freedom. They only think they do, but in fact they can't handle freedom. What they really want is authority. They want certainty, not the painful process of making difficult choices and wondering if they have done the right thing. We have spent 1,500 years, the cardinal tells Jesus, teaching people that religion means letting us tell them what they may or may not do, and we're not going to let you come and mess that up.

I can believe that a lot of people find making moral choices an intimidating process. But I also believe that God wants us to grow up and take on that burden. There is no going back to the Garden of Eden, to a time before we ate the fruit and developed a conscience. There is no going back to the days of childhood, before we learned about right and wrong, back when the only way to be "good" was to be obedient. God has slammed that gate shut behind us.

A second reason for rooting one's life in a posture of unquestioning obedience is that it lets you off the hook. Nothing you do wrong is your fault. You were only following orders. If we do something because God commanded us to, then nobody can blame us. They can only blame God. In his classic work *Varieties of the Religious Experience*, William James cites a 15th Century Spanish monk who writes in his journal, "I know that when I die, I will go to heaven because I have never done anything of my own free will but only followed the instructions of my superiors. If I have ever sinned, the sin is not mine but theirs." Excuse me for thinking that that is not an impressive example of mature religion. That reduces us to the moral level of children and pets, for whom "being good" means being obedient, doing what you are told. I think that for a great many people, there is a longing to go back to being a child again, not being held responsible for what you do. But it seems to me that is the opposite of authentic religion. In my understanding of religion, responsibility is one of the hallmarks of a human being.

That is why Judaism invented the Bar Mitzvah, to say to young people as they come of age, "You're not a child any more. It's time for you to take responsibility for what you do." And that is why I admired the late Simon Wiesenthal, the Nazi hunter who spent the last fifty years tracking down elderly Nazis, not because he thirsted for revenge but because he paid them the compliment of seeing even Nazis as human beings, and as human beings, being responsible for what they did.

When God tells Abraham to substitute a sheep on the altar, I would like to think that was God's way of saying to him, "Abraham, don't be a sheep. Don't define piety as simply following. That's what you are up here to sacrifice. I summoned you in the beginning because I saw you as someone who was willing to say "No" to things that were asked of you, that you thought were wrong. Don't stop doing that just because you've become a follower of Mine"

I suspect many of you can see where this sermon is heading. We are living at a time when terrible things are being done and justified in the name of religion. They are done by Muslims on Israeli school buses and British subways. They are done by Christians at family planning clinics. They are done by Jews in disputes about the future borders of Israel. It's not the first time in human history, but it's the first time in recent history and that is one reason why we find it horrifying. It's as if the Middle Ages, the religious wars, the Inquisition were returning. You hear a lot of people saying that religion is the problem, that too many people are drunk on religion. Religion, they claim, gives too many people a sense of certainty, the confidence that they are right and everyone else is wrong, that they are God's agents and those who disagree with them are God's enemies.

For Ivan Karamazov in the Dostoevsky novel organized religion *is* the problem. It represents the disastrous conjunction of people's need to be told what to do and some leaders' thirst for power, the power to tell others what to do. I disagree. I think the problem is not too much religion but not enough religion, not enough of the kind of religion that was revealed to Abraham on Mt. Moriah, the kind of religion that is grounded in God's having given us a conscience to know the difference between right and wrong and God's wanting us to grow up and use that conscience, the kind of religion that would say to suicide bombers and abortion clinic bombers, as I would like to think God said to Abraham on Mt. Moriah, "Where did you ever get the idea that killing people was the will of God?"

Now when I ask rhetorically "where did you ever get the idea that killing people was the will of God?" I realize that some people could say to me, "I got it from the Bible. I got it from all those places where God mandates the killing of Midianites and Amalekites, all those passages in which we are commanded to kill people for violating the Sabbath or showing disrespect to their parents. I find a lot of that in the Torah, but I don't find anywhere in the Torah where it says that if you don't like this commandment, you don't have to do it."

As Jews who revere the Torah as the Word of God, how do we respond to that? How do we relate to passages in the Torah that offend our conscience, whether it is about killing Canaanite women and children and destroying their religious sites, or about condemning gay love or limiting the role of women in society? I remember my teacher, Abraham Joshua Heschel, once citing the verse from the Torah, "These are the laws and commandments which you shall do, *v'chay bahem*, and live by them," and interpreting those last words, *v'chay bahem* to mean "and live *with* them." He asked "what if the Torah summons us to do something that we can't live with, something our consciences cannot abide?" Is it possible for human beings to be more moral than God? Is it conceivable for us to say "No" to the word of God on moral grounds and still be loyal Jews?

Let me suggest that when we are bothered by what we find in the Torah or elsewhere in Judaism, it is not a matter of our passing judgment on God's word. It is not a matter of our judging the Torah by the moral standards of the 21st Century and finding it inadequate. What we are doing at that moment is responding to one passage in the Torah with a conscience that has been formed by the Torah as a whole. We are calling the Torah to witness against itself, citing the loftiest passages of the Torah to supersede some of its earlier and less impressive verses.

There are places in the Torah that reflect the limited scientific and historic knowledge of its time, but the Torah as a whole, Judaism as a whole, is marked by an unflinching commitment to Truth. We don't have to be afraid of what astronomers learned about the relation of the earth and the sun, by what Darwin learned about the evolution of species or what Freud learned about the darkest recesses of the human soul. If it's true, there is room for it in our understanding of Torah. *Emet*, Truth is one of the names of God. *HaRahaman*, the Compassionate One, is one of the names of God. The same Torah that on one page seeks to exclude people – women, gays, gentiles, the physically handicapped – is the same Torah that on page after page speaks so eloquently about the innate dignity of each and every human being.

A colleague of mine, who is a member of the committee charged with coming up with a Conservative policy on the question of ordaining gay men and women as rabbis, told me that one of the more traditional members of the committee said to him, "My heart goes out to those young men and women. I respect the legitimacy and the honesty of their feelings. I have no doubt that they would be fine rabbis. But what can I do when the Torah tells me that they are sinners?" Well, maybe what he can do is to ask himself, as Abraham had to ask himself, which is the authentic voice of God, the voice of compassion or the voice of exclusion?

My friends, the story of the near-sacrifice of Isaac begins with the words, *Vay'hi achar had'varim ha-eleh v'ha-elohim nissa et Avraham*, It happened at that time that God tested Abraham. I don't believe that the test was to see if Abraham would obey without question, without hesitation, no matter how morally outrageous the demand was. I believe the test was to see whether Abraham's conscience had matured to the point where it could distinguish between the authentic and the inauthentic voice of God. Which voice, the voice that said "Kill" or the voice that said "Stop and Don't Do It," was more in keeping with everything he had previously known about God? And I believe that God is testing us today. God is looking for Muslims who will say "No, I have read the Koran and the God I pray to five times a day is a God who cherishes life and not death." God is looking for Christians who will say "No, the Christianity to which I have pledged my soul is about whom I am required to love, not about whom I am entitled to hate." And God is looking for Jews who will say "No, if I am asked to do things in the name of the Torah that violate the spirit of the Torah, things that make it hard for me to be the kind of person the Torah wants me to be, I will not do them."

At a turbulent, confusing time like the one we are living in, a time that makes it so tempting to hate people, a time when choices are so complicated that we crave someone to tell us what to do because it is so hard to decide for ourselves, I believe that God is testing us even as He tested Abraham, to see if we have learned to recognize God's authentic voice in the midst of so many competing voices and competing ideologies. May God grant that we be up to the challenge of passing that test. AMEN

A GENERATION AGO,

out of our love for this country which

welcomed us and promised us freedom,

we thought the nicest thing we could do

for America in return was to shed

our differences and become like everybody

else. We meant well but we were wrong.

America already had enough people

who were like everybody else.

Knowing Our Own Strength

On the 100th anniversary of the Statue of Liberty, Rosh HaShanah 1987

I don't know how you reacted to the Rededication Weekend for the Statue of Liberty last July fourth, but I loved it. I mean, what better way to celebrate America as a land of opportunity for all than to have two hundred Elvis Presley impersonators singing together? That must have been what the poet Emma Lazarus had in mind when she wrote about "the wretched refuse of your teeming shore."

But seriously, I was very moved by the ceremonies, as an American and as a Jew. I think the Statue of Liberty, placed in New York harbor in 1886, the time and place that saw the greatest Jewish immigration to these shores, has always meant something special to the American Jew. It welcomed my parents when they came from Eastern Europe in the early years of this century, and I suspect it was there to greet the parents and grandparents of many of you. And even for those of us whose families came to these shores before 1886 or arrived at ports of entry other than New York City, I think the Statue of Liberty meant something special for us and our families. It was America's official answer to a question that almost no American Jew can avoid asking, "Do we really belong here?"

Whether we studied Jewish history over the two thousand years of the Diaspora or whether we heard stories of discrimination from our parents and grandparents, or even if we had been called names on our way home from school or overheard jokes at our expense, we knew how fragile and insecure a Jewish minority had been wherever our people had lived.

But the Statue of Liberty represented the promise that America would be different; that even if there were individual bigots and bullies, the official American position was that America welcomed immigrants; and that all who came in search of freedom would be accepted here.

"Do we really belong here?" That's a much older Jewish question than we realize. It goes back beyond the immigration from Europe, even beyond the destruction of the Temple and the dispersion of the Jews nineteen centuries ago. It goes back to the earliest days of the Jewish people, to Abraham. In a passage that comes immediately after the chapter we read on Rosh HaShanah, Abraham's wife Sarah dies and he has to arrange for a burial plot for her. He says to his Canaanite neighbors, in whose midst he has lived for years, *ger v'toshav anochi imachem*, I am a stranger and a resident in your midst. Will you help me buy the cave of Machpela from its current owner? The Rabbis comment on those words that Abraham was not sure whether he was a *toshav*, a full-fledged resident of the community after all the years he had lived there, or whether he was a *ger*, a stranger among them. Was he one of them because he had lived there so long, because he had contributed so much to the community, even though his ways and beliefs were different? Or despite all that, did they persist in seeing him as a stranger?

It sounds a lot like the ambivalence I have heard from members of this congregation, and from other American Jews, about running for public office, or being conspicuous in other ways. Are we really fully accepted; are we just like anybody else? Or is there something fragile and tentative about the status we have achieved? Do we have to watch our step and be careful not to offend, not to become too conspicuous? No Christians reacted to Aldrich Ames getting caught spying for the Russians the way so many Jews reacted to Jonathan Pollard being caught spying for Israel. It's like the ambivalence we feel when a Pat Robertson or one of the other television preachers calls on Americans to declare the United States a Christian nation. Like Abraham, we've been here a long time. We've paid our dues; we've served in the armed forces. And we are still not sure if we are fully welcome.

If you are surprised that Abraham was already asking that question four thousand years ago, you'll be even more surprised at the answer his Canaanite neighbors gave him. They didn't say "You're welcome here because we are very generous about tolerating minorities." They didn't say "Hey, people are all the same; we don't care what a man believes as long as he's a good neighbor." They said *N'si Elohim atta b'tocheinu*, You are God's representative in our midst. They said, we are grateful that you are here because you make our community a different community by your presence, because you have brought God to our midst.

There is a phenomenon, a rather widespread psychological phenomenon, of people not knowing their own strength, of feeling weak and vulnerable because they are so familiar with their own faults and weaknesses, but have no idea how powerful they really are. Friends of mine who are therapists, for example, will describe a young woman in treatment who will complain constantly that she can't be happy because her mother tyrannizes her. Her mother is always putting her down. She makes plans and her mother forces her to change them. Her mother is always making her feel guilty. She paints this portrait of her mother as an ogre, a domineering tyrant who won't let her grow up and be her own person.

Then one day the therapist gets to meet the mother, and she turns out to be a frail, sick old lady, in no shape to tyrannize anyone, desperately afraid of being abandoned and left alone in her old age. If she won't let go, it's not because she wants to control. It's because she is afraid that if she doesn't clutch and hold on, her daughter who has so many more interesting things to do will leave her to fend for herself. The mother sees only her own weaknesses and her daughter's power. She doesn't realize that, old and feeble as she may be, she still has the power to turn her daughter into a little girl again, anxious for her approval. The daughter sees only her own weakness, and doesn't realize how helpless her mother is against her power to stay away and keep the grandchildren at a distance. And what the therapist has to do is bring each of them to appreciate her own power, so that she will feel less threatened by the strength of the other.

When you understand how that works, you will understand better the convoluted and highly emotional relationship between Jews and blacks in the United States. To be a Jew is to be painfully aware of the volcano of Anti-Semitism simmering just below the surface of American life. From Lyndon LaRouche to a Sunday School teacher in Georgia describing the crucifixion to a Kansas farmer whose land has just been foreclosed by the bank, the reference to the Jew as villain is never far out of reach. To be a Jew in America is to be conscious of the fact that there are not that many really good jobs or really good colleges, and if you are Jewish, there will always be extra barriers placed between you and them. To be a Jew is to realize the insecurity of the American Jew.

But the American black, looking at the Jewish community, doesn't see vulnerability. He sees us as part of the establishment, comfortably middle class or better, overwhelmingly prominent in suburban life, in the arts and science, in entertainment and industry. To him, it seems that we have not only become part of the American mainstream, we have risen to the top. And if we are afraid of him — afraid of black power politically when it comes to quotas, so much more sensitive to the remarks of a Jesse Jackson than any other well-established group, and afraid of him physically in terms of urban crime, — he can't understand that. Which weapon, after all, will help you get further in life, a six-inch switchblade or a six-figure bank account? Once again, each of us knows his own weakness and the other's strength better than we know our own strength and the other's vulnerability.

To be an Israeli Jew is to be reminded daily of your country's vulnerability. To be an Israeli Jew is to teach your five-year-old daughter not to pick up toys in the street because they might be booby trapped, to teach her to look for suspicious packages on the way to school. To be an Israeli Jew is to have your business or educational plans interrupted by military reserve duty every year well into your forties, and to turn on the radio every hour to make sure that no new disaster has occurred. It is to understand that your enemies can lose five or six wars and still go back to plan the next one, but that if you lose even once, there will no longer be a Jewish state anywhere in the world.

But to be an Arab is to look across the border and see an army that has been undefeated in five wars in forty years. It is to look up in the sky and see the third mightiest air force in the world flying overhead. It is to read about the financial and political support the United States seems ready to give Israel in almost unlimited quantities. And the Arab can't understand why the Israeli is afraid of him, why Israel, apparently so invulnerable, needs security guarantees from the likes of him.

We feel insecure, we act insecure, sometimes because we don't know our own strength. Like Abraham, we don't know if we are being tolerated or if we have actually gained acceptance and equality. So there are things we are reluctant to do, and things we are afraid to ask for, only to find out, as Abraham did, that people have been counting on us to do those things all along.

What is the image of the American Jew in the eyes of our non-Jewish neighbor? We know what the anti-Semites think of us, and we know what the Christian missionaries think of us. But the average American is neither a missionary nor an anti-Semite. What does he or she think of us? I suspect they see us as a lot stronger, a lot more secure and less vulnerable than we see ourselves, and in some cases, they see us much as Abraham's Canaanite neighbors saw him, as *N'si Elohim b'tocheynu*, the embodiment of God's presence in their midst.

A valuable resource in determining that would be the ten thousand people every year who become Jewish by choice. Born gentile, they convert to Judaism, sometimes to marry into a Jewish family, sometimes to complete a personal spiritual pilgrimage of their own, and occasionally to do both at once. I meet a new candidate for the conversion process about once a month, and in the course of the intake interview, I ask them what they already know about Jews and Judaism. Granted, they may not be typical American Christians. There are very few anti-Semites or evangelicals among them. Some of them probably had a more favorable than average opinion of Judaism even before they became romantically involved with someone Jewish. But they do represent a cross section of gentile America in their religious, educational and even geographic background, so what they tell me, I think, is significant. And what is even more amazing, they all tell me the same thing, and I think that makes their testimony even more valuable.

The first thing that strikes them about Judaism is its moral seriousness. We are a people that cares, a people that speaks out in the name of social and economic justice. We care about this world. Where others narrow their focus to their own salvation, leaving a sinful world behind, or where others balance the unfairness of this world with the promise of a perfect life in the hereafter, Jews are so outraged at this world's unfairness that we knock ourselves out to do something about it, to help the poor, the starving, the oppressed. Barely more than two percent of the American population (which nobody believes, because we are so conspicuous), we are over represented in almost all efforts to make this world more nearly resemble the Kingdom of God, the decent society God summoned us to build.

Moral seriousness - we are among the very few American groups willing to put the well being of all America ahead of their own self-interest. As Milton Himmelfarb put it after the last election, Jews are still the only people who earn like Episcopalians and vote like Puerto Ricans. Consistently, we don't vote for the Jewish candidate, or even the most pro-Israel candidate (although we will vote against the candidate who seems unreliable on Israel). Consistently, we vote for the candidate most likely to make ours a more decent and more compassionate society.

We are a charitable people, and America knows it and counts on us for it. Foolish people still make jokes about the Jewish craving for money, but people who know what's going on in American life know that no university and no museum, no medical research and no civil rights organization can balance its budget without Jewish support. Two percent of the population, we make America a more generous, more compassionate society by our generosity.

The other big thing these non-Jews considering becoming Jewish always tell me about is the warmth and closeness of the Jewish family. We've grown up with it so much that we take it for granted. We assume all families hug and kiss and fight and argue over trivialities. We assume all parents contemplate taking out an ad in the Globe when their child brings home a straight-A report card. Philip Roth has even enlightened us on how smothering and destructive that kind of love is. But when you've lived outside and seen it from the outside, you envy it. You know how rare and life-enhancing that kind of warmth is in a cold world.

In an America where the family is falling apart, people are looking to us to teach them how to be a family. In an America where everybody is increasingly looking out for himself, people see the Jewish community as a rare and glowing instance of people still feeling they have obligations to each other. They know what we do for Israel, they know what we do for Soviet Jewry, and if from time to time they talk about it in accents of resentment, I think a lot of it is envy. They wish they had somebody who belonged to them that way. *Fiddler on the Roof* wasn't a long-running hit solely because of synagogue theatre parties. All of American responded to something authentic in Tevya's family that they found missing in their own.

The key word, I think, is "authentic." Outsiders see the Jewish community as an authentic community, where people really care about each other and about the world they live in. They see the Jewish family as a real family, deeply entangled with each other's lives, not an accidental concatenation of semi-independent individuals sharing the same address. And they understand how much they need that kind of authenticity.

The problem is, those qualities are true of Judaism. I'm not sure they are true of American Jews. I'm not sure our families are still that different from other families. I wonder if we haven't lost the art of being generous, giving to the needy first and then seeing if there is enough left for a winter vacation instead of the other way around.

And the reason for the change is that we don't know our own strength. The first generation of Jews that moved out to the suburbs was so concerned about being accepted, about fitting in. We were convinced that in order for our new neighbors to like us, we had to persuade them that we were just like them. So we set out to abandon everything that had made us unique. One sarcastic comment from a Little League coach and we decided our child didn't really have to go to Junior Congregation on Saturday mornings. One impatient remark by a ballet teacher was enough to convince us that regular attendance at Religious School wasn't all that much of a priority. One funny look from a stranger at a barbecue, and we decided that keeping kosher was a relic from another age. Like Abraham, we saw ourselves as both *ger* and *toshav*, not sure if we really belonged out here or were we still here on approval. And in the process, we missed out on an important truth. Our new neighbors didn't want imitation gentiles. Why should they when they could find so many real ones so easily? Our strength had always been that we were a people who took God's word seriously, no matter what people said about us, but suddenly we could see only our weakness and we forgot our strength. We couldn't quite believe that America would really let us be ourselves, and when like Abraham's neighbors, they not only told us they would, when they told us they needed us to do that, we were more than a little bit astonished.

Let me give you an example. Exactly a month ago today, an important figure in American Jewish history died. Do you know to whom I'm referring? Hank Greenberg, the Hall of Fame first baseman for the Detroit Tigers in the 1930s and '40s. He was the first Jewish superstar athlete. The obituary notices last month spoke of the year he hit 58 home runs, of his record for runs batted in, of his being the first ballplayer to earn one hundred thousand dollars a year.

But none of the ones I read included my favorite Hank Greenberg story. One year when the High Holy Days came early and the pennant race ran late, Greenberg faced the dilemma of playing or not playing a key game on Yom Kippur. Greenberg, needless to say, was not a very observant Jew. He felt an obligation to his teammates to play, but at the same time felt an obligation to himself, to his own authenticity, to take the day off. Most Jews encouraged him to play, because they were afraid the non-Jewish world would resent it if the team lost because he wasn't there, and in their understanding of Judaism there was nothing more important than not offending the non-Jewish world. Ultimately he decided not to play. He went to shul instead. And to everyone's surprise, all of Detroit and all of America applauded his decision.

The Hearst newspaper in Detroit, ordinarily no friend of the Jews, put his picture on the front page with the headline *L'Shana Tova*. The lesson, it seems to me, was this: America cheers for winners but America respects people of integrity more. There is always a winner. Every year, somebody wins, sometimes by talent, sometimes by cheating, sometimes by good luck. There are lots of success stories, accounts of people making it to the top by not caring about anything except making it to the top. But there are all too few stories about people who cared more about being true to themselves than they did about winning. We win a place in America's heart by daring to be true to our authentic selves.

My friends, where is America in 1986? America is uncomfortable with the kind of society it is becoming. America is embarrassed by its music and its movies, by its poverty and its urban crime. America is desperately looking for some sort of moral guidance. That is why people tune in to the mindless bigotry of Jimmy Swaggart and the arrogance of Pat Robertson. That is why people with college degrees are turning to the fundamentalist churches and the Lubavitcher shtiblach. They are looking for moral seriousness, for spiritual authenticity. America needs people to show it how to be a decent, compassionate society again. America wants to be good, but doesn't know how. And we let America down when we are afraid to be the people we are supposed to be.

We don't know our own strength. We don't realize how much people are depending on us to be authentic Jews, to change the air and show the way. They are depending on us to show them what a family looks like, what a community looks like, what generosity looks like. But when they look to us, they see us trying to look like them. And that is what they resent. That is when they feel betrayed and let down.

A generation ago, two generations ago, out of our love for this country, which welcomed us and promised us freedom, we thought that the nicest thing we could do for America in return was to shed our differences in the melting pot and become like everybody else. We would change our names, we would change our habits. We would learn to drink and cheat and run around, just like real

Americans. And we were so flattered when somebody said to us "you don't look Jewish." We did that, not because we loved Judaism less; we felt very loyal to Judaism. But we did it because we loved America more, and we thought that was what America wanted. We meant well, but we were wrong. America already had enough people who were like everybody else.

Today, out of our love for this country, which has treated us so well, we understand that the nicest thing we can do for America is to be good Jews, to be our authentic selves. The American soul is not enriched by imitation. It is enriched by people of integrity and moral seriousness. It respects authentic people, people who know who they are and bear it proudly. More than respect, it envies them. If we would be bold enough to lay claim to the strength that is ours, strength we did not know we had, the strength that comes from being yourself and not feeling you have to wear a borrowed mask, then we would hear our neighbors say with gratitude and admiration, as Abraham heard his neighbors say, *N'si Elohim atta b'tocheynu,*" You are the people who bring God down to earth in our midst. You are the people for whom we lift the lamp beside the golden door."

REMIND US OF WHAT

it feels like to really be alive,

to discover anew that there are people

who love us and care about us,

and to realize what a miracle that is.

REMIND US TO LIVE

Rosh HaShanah 1998

Before there was Rosh HaShanah, before these early fall days were known as the High Holy Days, before we had formed the habit of calling the first day of the month Tishre the Jewish New Year and the birthday of the world, the biblical name for this holiday was *yom teruah*, the day of sounding the shofar. The shofar is what is unique about today's service. Oh, the prayers are longer and some of the words are different, but those are matters of degree. The sounding of the shofar is what is unique and special about today.

And that's important, because while the prayers of the Rosh HaShanah service are addressed to God, the sound of the shofar is meant for us to hear. It's a wake-up call, an alarm clock; as if God were saying to us, "Don't just plead with Me for a year of life. I'm giving you life; what are you doing with it?"

Zachreinu l'hayyim. melech hafetz ba-hayyim, remember us for life, O King who desires life... or maybe the prayer means; Remind us to live, O God who cherishes life and wants His creatures to live. Remind us of what it feels like to be truly alive, because we feel it sometimes and we forget it so often. We pray for life, but so often we drift through life, sleepwalking through our days, and we need the alarm clock shrillness of the shofar to wake us out of our stupor.

In that lovely little book that became a number one best-seller, *Tuesdays With Morrie,* the account of a Brandeis University graduate who goes back to visit his favorite professor who is dying, the professor has this to say: So many people walk around with a meaningless life. They seem half-asleep, even when they are busy doing things they think are important. This is because they are chasing the wrong things. The way you get meaning into your life is to devote yourself to loving others, devote yourself to your community, and devote yourself to creating something.

What is the sound of the shofar? The first call of the shofar is *tekiah*, the summons to human connections. There is a verse in the Torah, in the Book of Numbers (10:7), that says: When you want to bring people together, sound the *tekiah*. And it is through connecting with other people that we bring life to our existence. You can't be a Jew all by yourself. You need other Jews, you need a minyan, you need a congregation. And you can't be a fully realized human being all by yourself, cutting yourself off from others, judging them, rejecting them, withdrawing from them, plotting to use them but never really connecting with them.

There is perhaps no time that we feel as alive as when we discover that somebody loves us. It's one of those moments you never forget. The whole world is different. Colors are brighter. Sunshine is warmer. Think of that classic movie scene of Gene Kelly singing in the rain, not minding the rain and the puddles that the rest of us complain about, because he's in love. Being loved validates our lives, because human beings were not meant to live in isolation. We were meant to share our lives with others.

When Martin Buber, the great Jewish philosopher and theologian would be asked, "Where is God?" Buber was wise enough not to give the cliché answer "God is everywhere," or to claim that God is found in synagogues, in churches, in holy people. Buber would say, "God is found in relationships." We realize our humanity; we become convinced that God is real, when we connect with other people.

We feel so good, so alive when we know that we are loved, but we so soon come to take it for granted. It's a miracle, but because we live with it every day, we soon stop seeing the miraculous nature of it. In the same way that we get on an airplane and instead of marveling at the fact that we can fly safely at 600 miles an hour, we complain about the food, the crowding, the delays, — in that same way, we come home to our families and instead of marveling at the fact that we have families to come home to, that there are people who belong to us, who want to share their lives with us, we shrug, we find fault, we take them for granted. That's why we need the *tekiah,* the blast of the shofar, to remind us of how blessed we are to be surrounded by people who care about us.

I should emphasize that when I talk about the joy of knowing that you are loved, I don't mean to limit it to the love between a husband and a wife. There are many people today who don't have spouses. Some are single, some are widowed, some are divorced. But I would hope that there is no one here who can't look at his or her life and find people who cherish you, people who care about you. And we realize that is what makes our lives worthwhile.

We pray to God for a year of life, and God says to us: "What is it you're asking for? Is it only a year of survival, a year of eating and sleeping and watching television and paying your bills?" Or is it a year of feeling alive, relishing every day, recapturing that sense of wondrousness that you remember from times when you realized that someone liked you, cherishing the miracle that there are people in your life who belong to you? *Tekiah.* The shofar sounds its wake-up call, reminding us to live, to stop taking for granted the miraculous fact that people like us, tolerate us, care about us. It summons us to love them and to bless them for loving us.

The second call of the shofar is *shevarim,* the broken note, the plaintive articulation of all the brokenness in our lives, the bereavements and the disappointments, the people taken from us whom we miss at this season and throughout the year, the dreams that didn't work out and will probably never work out. *Shevarim,* the broken note, issuing from and echoing in a thousand broken hearts.

How can the sound of grieving and disappointment be a call to life? First, because death and the fear of death teach us the preciousness of life. Just last week, I was speaking in Cleveland at an event organized by a local hospice. As part of the program, a hospice volunteer spoke of what working with people at the end of their lives has taught her. She said, "Preparing people for death has taught me the preciousness of life, how I have to be grateful for every day I have".

How often do we find ourselves plodding through our daily routines, and suddenly a phone call tells us of someone we care about being taken ill, being hospitalized, getting a bad report on a biopsy. It jolts us out of our routine and reminds us of what is truly important. And we, whose days were so busy and so full of obligations, manage to find time to do what we realize we need to do.

It is only because life is precious that death is tragic. Otherwise death would just be a statistic, the way of all flesh. The message that cries out to us from the empty seats at our holiday tables is that life is too short to be petty, life is too precious to be squandered, life is too fragile to be handled thoughtlessly. Some people look at the world we live in and say: Life is uncertain, so what's the point of living? What's the point of taking it seriously when the more seriously you take it, the more likely it is to break your heart?

But Judaism would teach us to say: Life is uncertain, so cherish every day you have. Take no day for granted. Don't put off the good deed, the kind word, the phone call of reconciliation. There is no guarantee that what you don't do today will be there for you to do tomorrow.

Over the years, I've heard many explanations of the Mourners' Kaddish, what it means and why we say it. But this summer, I ran across one I had never heard before. As you know, the Mourners Kaddish is not about death. It's not about mourning. It's a prayer that praises God for the world that God has given us. And one commentator suggests that we ask the mourners to recite it to emphasize gratitude for the person's life, for what he or she added to the world, rather than grief for the person's absence. It is the life that mattered; the death was only punctuation. *Shevarim,* the cry of the broken heart, is a tribute to life, to how much a single life can mean, not a lament for death.

That's one of the messages from the shofar sound of *shevarim.* But there is another. Kahlil Gibran has a line in his little book *The Prophet,* "The deeper a groove sorrow carves in you, the more joy you can contain." And the Hassidic master the Kotzker Rebbe used to say, "There is nothing as whole as a broken heart." It is through pain and heartbreak that we learn how to feel. When our hearts break, they create an opening for all sorts of emotion to rush in. When our souls purge themselves of old hopes and dreams that never happened, they create a space for new dreams, new dimensions of self-understanding. The heart that refuses to break has become so calloused that it is immune to all feeling.

One of the saddest things you have taught me over the thirty years that I served here is how hard it is for so many of you to celebrate. So many people know how to have fun, but don't know how to elevate it to the experience of joy, the kind of feeling that makes life worthwhile and leaves us feeling empty and cheated when we can't achieve it.

I remember a story that came out of Israel's victory in the Six Day War in June of 1967. One of the first Israeli soldiers to liberate the Old City of Jerusalem and stand at the Kotel, the Western Wall, told a reporter afterward "For the first time in my life, I wanted to pray and I didn't know how." I would be reminded of that story several times a year when I was Rabbi of this congregation.

The parents of a 13-year-old boy or girl would plan the Bar Mitzvah, and for maybe the first time in their lives, they want to celebrate. They want to express their gratitude to God for having successfully brought a child to this milestone but they don't know how. So for the Bar Mitzvah, they plan a party, and maybe it has a football theme or a soccer theme or a ballerina theme.

But there is nothing about a child taking his or her first steps into adolescent responsibility. There is nothing about the moral demands that young person will soon be facing, and how the parents feel about letting their child enter that world without them. There is nothing about the parents standing on the threshold of middle age, now that they have a teenager (nothing will age a parent faster than that), nothing about their depending on this child for their immortality, to continue what their lives have been about. And when it is over, there are a lot of presents to sort out and a lot of bills to pay and a lot of people saying, "we had a wonderful time," but there is no sense that a once-in-a- lifetime transition has just taken place. There was no sense that the parents were alive to the miracle of a child turning a comer in his or her life.

The parents of a bride plan a wedding, and because their souls are so inexperienced at celebrating, because they want to feel something special but don't have the emotional vocabulary to do that, what do they do? They hire the loudest band they can find, so that they will never find themselves alone with their inarticulate souls in the silence.

That helps me understand the phenomenon of teenage girls going to see the movie "Titanic" fourteen or fifteen times. They don't go for the movie; they must know the movie by heart by now. They don't go hoping for a happier ending. They go in order to cry, because only when they cry can they be sure they are alive. I've had so many teenagers tell me they must be terrible people because they loved their grandparents but they didn't cry at their grandmother's funeral. That's why we need *shevarim*, to summon us to life, to move us to take off the armor and let ourselves feel.

For all those families who are planning a Bar Mitzvah this year, for all those looking forward to a wedding, for those fortunate couples who will be making a 25th or a 50th wedding anniversary, God pleads with us: Let the sound of the shofar, the broken notes of *shevarim,* break open your hearts, pierce the protective armor that spares you from feeling. Let the joy flow into your unprotected hearts, and be reminded of what it feels like to be alive and to thank God that you are.

The third of the shofar's notes, *teruah,* is understood to be the proclamation of God's sovereignty, hailing God as ruler of the world, like the heralds' trumpets that announce the king, like the Marine band playing "Hail to the Chief." Now the theme of God's sovereignty, the idea that God rules the world, is a major part of our Rosh HaShanah prayers, and it operates at two very different levels. Sometimes the pronouncement that God is King asks us to bow in awe of the divine majesty. In just a few minutes, when we turn back to the prayerbook and resume the service, we will open the Ark, and the Cantor and I, as surrogates for the congregation, will bow before the awesome majesty of God. That's one dimension of it.

The second is in some ways the opposite of the first. We look out at this world and it doesn't look like God is in charge of it. We see hurricanes and earthquakes and tidal waves. We read about high school students murdering their classmates, and armies on four of the seven continents carrying out mass murders as if the lessons of the Holocaust had never been learned. We see disease and death, crime and poverty. And despite it all, we come to shul on Rosh HaShanah. We sound the shofar and insist that this is God's world. We find meaning amidst the chaos. We find goodness despite the cruelty. We cherish the light instead of cursing the darkness.

I think that's what it means to sound the *teruah* and proclaim God as ruler of the world. It's not to acknowledge God's greatness; it's to give God the benefit of the doubt. We ask God for so much on Rosh HaShanah. Our Father our King, grant us a year of life and health. Our Father our King, redeem Your people from oppression. Our Father our King, deal kindly with us despite our failings. And God asks only one thing of us in return: that we give God the benefit of the doubt, that we let the wonderful moments of our lives affirm our faith in God's world as readily as we let the terrible moments challenge it.

Often it's hard to believe that this is God's world because there is so much in the headlines that screams against it. But Rosh Ha-Shanah, and the shofar's call of *teruah,* would ask us to look beyond the headlines. The headlines tell us of a plane crash in Nova Scotia, leaving 211 people dead. The small print tells of hundreds of Canadian fishermen setting out in their boats to look for survivors. The headlines tell of massacres, small scale or large. The small print tells of individual acts of courage, of comfort: the closer we look, the more the presence of God becomes visible.

Teruah asks us in effect to vote for God as sovereign of the world, not because it makes a difference to God whether we vote for Him or not, He's not up for re-election this year, but because it makes a difference to us, to the way we live, to the way we respond to the good and bad news in the world, whether we see the world as a coherent, meaningful, livable place or not.

A few years ago, at a lecture I was giving, a woman asked the question: "How can I persuade my 9-year-old son to believe in God?" I told her, "If you'll pardon my saying so, that's the wrong question. The issue is not believing in God. You can't talk someone into believing. The question for Jewish parents and Jewish educators is how do you teach children to recognize God when they have met Him?"

How do you convince children and adults that God is real? Not with philosophical arguments. Rather, teach children that when they are sick and they get better, they have met God. When their favorite foods taste good and nourish their bodies and make them grow and make them strong, God has been active in their lives. When they go outdoors and it's a sunny day and the flowers are blooming and their hearts thrill to the beauty of the world, or when they wake up on a winter morning and there is a cover of clean, untrodden snow on the ground and they gasp with excitement at the view, they have met God who created a world where such things happen. When they do something wrong and they are caught and forgiven, and they learn that love is not tentative and will not be withdrawn and their souls nearly burst with relief, that is a religious moment. They have met God, who teaches us to love and to forgive.

When we have learned to look at the world and see God's fingerprints all over it, when we have learned to look within ourselves and sense the spirit of God moving us to be good, to be generous, to be compassionate, when we can gather on this day of the autumnal equinox, with exactly twelve hours of light and twelve hours of darkness, and learn to relish the daylight with gratitude and to welcome the darkness unafraid, then we will know that we are alive.

Zachreinu l'hayyim, melech hafetz ba'hayyim, Remind us to live, O God who desires life. Remind us of what it feels like to really be alive, to discover anew that there are people who love us and care about us and to realize what a miracle that is. Remind us that we have the strength and resilience to survive the worst that the New Year can possibly bring and the depth of soul to find abundant joy in the best days ahead so that we have no reason to be afraid of living into the New Year; and to see the face of God wherever we turn in this world.

Ashrei ha-am yod'ei teruah; Adonai, b'or panecha yehalechun. Happy are the people who know how to hear and understand the message of the shofar, for they shall spend all their days in the presence of God. AMEN.

A LOT HAS CHANGED from that Brooklyn
neighborhood that I remember so fondly,
but a lot of the change has been for the
better, and if some Faustian bargain had
given me the power to make time stand still
in 1955, it would have been a sin against
humanity to have done that.

Time Stands Still

Rosh HaShanah 1995

"There is a place where time stands still. Raindrops hang motionless in the air. Pendulums of clocks float mid-swing. Dogs raise their muzzles in silent howls. Pedestrians are frozen on the dusty streets, their legs cocked as if held by strings… For this is the center of time. From this place, time travels outward in concentric circles, at rest at the center, slowly picking up speed at greater diameters."

The passage is from a fascinating little book called *Einstein's Dreams* by Alan Lightman. The idea behind the book is that in 1905, Albert Einstein was working out his theory of relativity, which would revolutionize the way we think about time. He was so obsessed with it that at night he would dream about different worlds where time worked differently than it did in our universe.

For example, there is a world where time runs backwards, where people grow younger day by day, until they become infants and disappear into their mothers' wombs. There is a world where time runs in circles, and everything that ever happened happens again after a certain interval. There is a world where time passes more slowly at higher elevations, so that rich people build their houses on mountaintops and live on the top floors of those houses, so that time will pass more slowly and they will live a few hours longer than they would at sea level.

But the passage that remained with me after I had finished the book was the one I just cited, about a world where time stands still and nothing ever changes.

The author of *Einstein's Dreams* writes "Who makes the pilgrimage to the center of time? Parents with children, and people in love." And we understand him. There is a part of us that is deeply gratified by our children's growing up, that thrills to every new achievement. But there is also a part of us that knows what the passing of time will do to that relationship. The child who hugs us and needs us and dotes on our praise and makes us feel so smart and so irreplaceable today will evolve into the surly adolescent who slams doors and tells us how little we understand about life. The youngster who wakes up across the hall from us every morning will grow up and go off to college and make a life for himself or herself in another state. And part of us wants to say, "But it's so good now; why does it have to change? Why can't it just stay like this?"

Who travels to the still point in time? Parents with children and people in love. In our world, time moves on and we worry that time may not be kind to us or to the people we love. We're afraid that during the New Year, more of our conversations with our parents, our husbands, our wives will have to do with aches and pains and symptoms and doctors' appointments. And we want to say, "I'm not asking that things be the way they were when I was young, but could we just keep them the way they are now and not get any worse? Could we somehow make time stand still and not let the New Year come and take anything away from me?"

What after all is Netaneh Tokef, the prayer that is the emotional highlight of this day, if not a collective articulation of our fears about what the New Year might bring: "It is determined on Rosh HaShanah and confirmed on Yom Kippur, who shall live and who shall die, who by sword and who by illness ..." And we hear ourselves saying "If those are the coming attractions for the New Year, I'm not sure that's a movie I want to stay for."

We worry about our jobs, about our ability to keep on earning a living, in a world where things change so fast. Companies merge, companies downsize, companies move to another state. People's tastes change and they stop buying what was popular a year ago. So many things remind us that the foundations we've built our lives on, at home and at work, are a lot more fragile and a lot more vulnerable than we would like to think.

But one of the messages of Rosh HaShanah is that there is no stopping time, no way of making it stand still. Inexorably the New Year arrives and whether we like it or not, we have to tear the page off the calendar and go on to the next one.

Do you remember the legend of Faust, the man who sold his soul to the Devil in exchange for happiness in this life? The exact terms of the deal were that, if he ever found himself saying "Let this moment linger; it is so good," then the Devil could have his soul. When I read *Faust* in college, I thought I understood what that meant. I thought Faust was saying "If I could just have one moment when I could say 'This is great, it doesn't get any better than this', it would be worth my soul just to be that happy." But as I get older and I remember that Goethe was nearly eighty when he finished writing *Faust*, I wonder if it might really mean something else. I wonder if Faust was saying, "I would give my soul for the ability to make time stand still, the ability to take a moment and freeze it and never let it change, never let time come and take away that good feeling." And I wonder if the author of *Faust* was saying that the person who tries to make time stand still and keep the world from changing, loses his soul.

I've been trying to teach you for thirty years that religion means more than God taking attendance on Saturday mornings and checking on whether or not we've obeyed certain strange rules. Religion is the way we deal with the most basic issues of our lives, making sure we don't have to deal with them alone and sharing with us the wisdom of a hundred generations of thinking about those issues. If one of our basic concerns as we grow a year older is to wish that we could make time stand still because we are afraid of the future, afraid of what change will do to us, to our families, to our world, what answers does Judaism have for us?

Basically, Judaism tells us not to be afraid of the future, not because it guarantees the future will be good to us but because it wants to reassure us that we have the resources, the personal and the communal resources to cope with whatever the future has in store. Judaism's promise is not that it can keep us safe but that it can make us strong, strong enough to overcome whatever the New Year may bring.

It would tell us first not to be afraid of change because much of what changes, changes for the better. Not all change is loss; not all growth is malignant growth. I had occasion last spring to speak in a synagogue in Brooklyn, just a few blocks away from where I grew up. As I drove past the streets with the familiar names of my childhood, I found myself mourning the disappearance of that world I grew up in, a world of neighborhood shopping, flourishing synagogues on every block, safe subways, academically challenging public schools and the lights of Ebbets Field visible from our front porch during the baseball season. I found myself wishing there were some way I could have frozen time in the early 1950s and prevented that neighborhood from deteriorating into the decrepit, crime-ridden slum it has become.

But as I thought about it over the following few days, I realized I probably would not have wanted to go back to the past even if I could. First of all, it would have meant canceling out everything I've done in my life since then. But more than that. Yes, the corner grocer knew your name and would extend credit if you were short on cash, but the canned goods were dusty and the milk was one day away from turning sour and you didn't have the choice of products you have today. For a nickel, you could ride the subway, but getting out of the city was a long ordeal over poor roads by car, and plane travel was about as common as space travel today. If you got sick, there was so much less that doctors could do for you, and the air was so polluted that you had to wipe a layer of grime off the windowsill every morning. Mothers were expected to stay home with their children, or if they worked, they could be secretaries or schoolteachers and not much more than that. A lot has changed from that Brooklyn neighborhood of forty years ago that I remember so fondly, but a lot of the change has been for the better, and if some Faustian bargain had given me the power to make time stand still in 1955, it would have been a sin against humanity to have done that.

Judaism would remind us that change can be scary because it represents leaving the familiar and stepping out into something new. Judaism begins with Abraham leaving the home he grew up in for an unknown destination. It is the story of a band of slaves leaving Egypt for a life they can't imagine, and being so anxious at the prospect that every now and then, they are tempted to call it off and go back to Egypt.

Judaism understands that change is often painful, but that not all pain is bad. Sometimes the pain we feel is the result of growing and stretching. A colleague of mine remembers the day he took his daughter for her first day of kindergarten. As he left her there, anxious and fearful and trying hard not to cry, (he was all those things; his daughter was fine.) and closed the door behind him, because it was the High Holy Day season and he was writing his sermons, he thought of the symbolism of doors closing, ending one chapter of our lives and beginning a new one, and how we would never grow if we were afraid to close doors behind us, to leave the familiar and move into the unknown.

I remember telling a member of the congregation who was having problems with a teenager that giving birth to an adolescent can be as painful as giving birth to a newborn child. Cutting the strings that bind a growing child to his or her parents can be painful surgery for both parties, and there are moments when we might be tempted to shy away from the pain, to not grow up because it's safe at home and so scary out there.

But Judaism commands us to begin the New Year by re-reading the story of Adam and Eve on the first Sabbath of the Torah cycle, how God decreed that because we had gained knowledge of Good and Evil, because we now knew what was right and what was wrong in a way that other creatures could not know, we would find being a parent more painful than any other creature does. And we understand that like Adam and Eve, we have to be wise enough to let go, and like Abraham, our children have to be brave enough to go forth.

But more than anything else, Judaism speaks to those of us who might be tempted to make time stand still, and it says to us: "Don't be afraid." Don't be afraid, not because things won't change that much in the coming year. They may change dramatically. And not because the change won't hurt. It may hurt a lot. But don't be afraid of change because you're strong enough to handle it, and your religion is one of the things that makes you strong enough to handle it.

If the prayer Netaneh Tokef is our great cry of apprehension, of concern over what the New Year might take away from us, what is the prayerbook's answer to that cry? It comes in seven words of Hebrew at the end of Netaneh Tokef, *ut'shuvah ut'fillah ut'zedakah ma'avirin et ro'a hag'zerah*. Repentance, prayer and charity avert the severity of the decree. Notice how carefully that line is phrased. It doesn't say that repentance, prayer and charity avert the decree, that being religious will keep bad things from happening to you. If it said that, people would have noticed hundreds of years ago that it wasn't true. It says that they avert the *severity* of the decree. Bad things may happen to you but they won't hurt as much, because you will have learned to see yourself and to see the world around you in a way that keeps those misfortunes in perspective.

Prayer can make the bitter moments of the New Year hurt less. I remember years ago, a man came up to me and said "Rabbi, you know that since my father died, I've been coming to the minyan every night to say Kaddish. For the next month or so, I'll be traveling a lot on business. Some nights I'll be on a plane when it's time for the evening service. Some nights I'll be in a small town where there is no synagogue. Would it be a sin if I just said Kaddish by myself in my room?"

I told him "No, I think it would be the right thing to do. I know how important it is for you to say Kaddish for your father every day. Just don't lose sight of the fact that when you say Kaddish with a congregation, two very important things happen that don't happen when you say it by yourself. First, the other members of the congregation give you strength by welcoming you, by saying Amen to your prayer, and because several of them are mourners as well, they remind you that you're not the only one to whom this has happened.

"And the second thing is, you give them strength. When they see you in shul, when they hear the one person who has the most reason to be angry at God get up and affirm God, that does something for them. It banishes their fear that when they lose someone they love, they won't be able to handle it. It teaches them something about the resiliency of the human soul in the face of tragedy."

The discipline of prayer can't protect us from pain and sorrow. It can't prevent people from getting old, from getting sick. But it can avert the severity of the decree. It can make it hurt less.

And if we come to understand what *teshuvah*, repentance, really means, it can help us deal with adverse fate as well. I think the word "repentance" makes a lot of us uncomfortable because it has connotations of beating our breasts and groveling and saying "I'm no good, it's all my fault." But that's wrong. *Teshuvah*, repentance in Judaism, is really the opposite of that. It asks us to say "yes, I've done some things wrong, as everybody does. But that's not the essential me. The real me is capable of being good and strong and brave most of the time."

The unexpected success of the Red Sox this summer had me remembering the last time the Red Sox were in the World Series, in 1986. I don't know if you remember it, but we had problems starting Kol Nidre on time that year. The Red Sox were in a play-off game in California. If they lost, their season would be over. And people didn't want to leave for shul until the game had been decided. The Red Sox were losing with two out in the ninth inning, when California pitcher Donnie Moore gave up a home run to Dave Henderson that cost California the ballgame. Donnie Moore never got over that one mistake. He blamed himself for his team's losing. He kept wishing he could turn back the clock, do that one moment over again and do it differently. Two years later, he was traded. A year after that, he was out of baseball. Then, hopelessly depressed, he took his own life. He could never forgive himself for doing that one thing wrong.

Now contrast that with something that happened two-and-a half-years ago in a college basketball game. A 19-year-old sopho-more from Michigan, Chris Webber, made a mental mistake that cost his team the national championship. But unlike Donnie Moore, he didn't lose faith in himself. He said "that was a dumb thing to do, but it doesn't change the fact that I'm a good player." A year later, Chris Webber was the NBA's Rookie of the Year.

If we root our lives in goodness, in honesty, in charity, then even if the bad things that come our way are the result of bad decisions on our part, our sense of ourselves as good people will diminish the severity of what happens to us.

And if we form the habit of charity, of feeling the pain of other people and wanting to do something to help them, then our own problems will hurt us less, not only because we will be aware of how much suffering there is in the world, but also because we will have learned to see ourselves as people with the power to do something about it. We will see ourselves as people who act, not as passive victims.

My friends, the synagogue is not a place to escape from the real world. The synagogue is not a place for people who want things to remain the same and never change. The synagogue is where you learn what the world is really about, what really matters in this world, and how you armor yourself against the dangers the world poses.

And on Rosh HaShanah, the synagogue's message is "don't be afraid." Don't be afraid of change, of not being able to control things that are so important to you, not because life guarantees happy endings but because the right kind of life leaves you equipped to cope with whatever ending comes along. Don't be afraid that life may hurt, not because we can promise you that it won't hurt, but because faith and friends and self-esteem will make you strong enough to take it.

On Rosh HaShanah, the synagogue asks us to give up our fantasy to make time stand still. It asks us to give up our illusion that what we have today, we will have forever. And it asks us to give up our fear of the future. In their place, it offers us the way of *teshuvah, tefillah utzedakah,* the way of confidence, prayer and generosity, so that as the door of the old year closes behind us, we can enter the door that opens for us, and we can enter it unafraid.

WE COME TO SERVICES ON ROSH HASHANAH
and we virtually challenge God: "Reveal
Yourself! Make something happen so that
I'll know You're there." And God says to us,
"You want to see Me? Go out and do godly
things. Help the poor and comfort the
grieving. Make your community a better place,
and then go home and look in the mirror.
That's as close as you will ever come to
seeing what God looks like."

Yearning to See God

Rosh HaShanah 2003

Those of us who are here early enough on these two mornings of Rosh HaShanah are treated to two stories from the Torah that parallel each other in some interesting ways. The reading this morning tells of how Hagar, Abraham's concubine, was sent away with her young son Ishmael because Abraham and Sarah were afraid that Ishmael was having a bad influence on Isaac. They lose their way in the desert, they are out of food and water and the boy is about to die of thirst when an angel appears and points Hagar to a nearby well. Their lives are saved and Hagar names the well *Be'er L'Hai Ro'i*, the well of the living God who sees me, or as I would interpret it, "at the bottom of the well, at the lowest point of my life, when I felt helpless and abandoned, I met God and learned that God cares about me."

Then tomorrow we read that story that defies all understanding: God commands Abraham to take his beloved son Isaac, born to him after years of yearning, and offer him as a sacrifice on a nearby mountain. Abraham is about to comply when, at the last moment, an angel intervenes and tells him to stop and not harm the child. God tells Abraham that because he has shown such faith, he and his descendants will play an important role in the religious history of the world. Abraham calls the place where that happened *Bahar Adonai Yera'eh*, the mountain where God is seen, or as I would interpret it, "at the high point of my life, the day when my child was returned to me safe and unharmed and I learned that I would be successful in my dream of changing the world, I felt I had seen the face of God."

Why did the Sages of two thousand years ago ordain those particular stories to be read year after year on Rosh HaShanah? Maybe they did it because they understood something about why people come to today's service.

Why do we come? Why are these the services for which we set out six hundred extra seats and set up a tent in the parking lot? Some of us come, I'm sure, because these prayers mean a lot to us. The words, the music, the memories, the experience of being in a large throng of Jews gathered for worship — that reaches us at a deep part of our souls.

Some of us come out of a lingering sense of obligation, a feeling that this is something we ought to do whether we enjoy it or not, what my teacher Mordecai Kaplan described as "observing the yahrzeit of our parents' religion." Some people, I suspect, come because they are afraid that something bad will happen to them if they don't come. Let me explain what I mean by that. I would hope that no member of this congregation literally thinks that if you are marked absent on Rosh HaShanah, you won't be inscribed in the Book of Life and as a result, something terrible will befall you during the year. I hope you don't believe that. But for some people, being Jewish is a marginal part of their daily identity. It doesn't really flavor their lives that much. But they understand that if they went to the office on Rosh HaShanah and Yom Kippur, they would be making a statement to themselves and to the people around them about the utter insignificance of being Jewish, a statement that they are not prepared to make. So they come.

But all those reasons cover only a part of the congregation. There is another reason why many of us come year after year. We come because we are hoping to meet God here. We want to meet God the way Hagar and Abraham met God. We want something to happen during these hours that will convince us that God is real beyond any doubt and that God cares about us.

Sometimes, every now and then, it happens and we walk out inspired. But most of the time we go home kind of disappointed. The service was fine, the rabbi and cantor did their tasks well, but where was God? I met my neighbors, I met the leaders of the congregation, but I'm not sure I met God. Why not? For one thing, Hagar and Abraham met God at the high points and low points of their lives, days when their children were in danger, days when their most desperate prayers were suddenly answered. At times like that, it's not hard to believe that God is real and cares about you. In much the same way, it's not that hard to sense the holiness, the religious dimension of a wedding, a birth, even of a funeral when religion works to heal even people who are not religious. But most of us don't live on mountaintops or at the bottom of wells in the desert. Most of us live most of our days at sea level, and our lives are marked by few triumphs and few dangers. We never seem to run into God there, and so we come to shul on these High Holy Days hoping they will in fact be days of High Holiness, hoping something extraordinary will happen and we will be able to walk out of the synagogue seeing the world differently than we did when we walked in.

It's not a new story. People have always longed to come face to face with God, to banish all doubts that God was real and not just something the authorities made up, like Santa Claus or the tooth fairy, to make us behave. Four months after the Israelites left Egypt and crossed the Red Sea, forty days after God gave our ancestors the Ten Commandments, the Israelites felt a desperate need to see God, to have tangible proof that God was still with them and had not abandoned them after leading them into the desert. Remember, these were people who had spent every day of their lives in Egypt, a highly visual, highly materialistic culture, with its pyramids and treasure houses. In Egypt, if something was real, you could see it. Dead people weren't simply remembered; they were kept around as mummies. The branch of mathematics in which Egypt excelled was not algebra or calculus or quadratic equations but geometry, the measurement of real things. No wonder the Israelites had trouble absorbing the idea that something can be real but you can't see it.

As long as Moses was around, they could look at Moses as an embodiment, an incarnation of God. For them, Moses was God in human form. He told them what God expected of them. He worked miracles, the Ten Plagues, splitting the Sea. But Moses was gone. He was on Mt. Sinai getting the details of the Torah beyond the Ten Commandments. Do you remember what the Israelites did? They fashioned a Golden Calf to represent the power and the glory of God. God was no longer an intellectual abstraction. Now they could see the God they were praying to. They could see that God was present in their midst.

God gets angry at them for turning Him into a thing, an idol. Moses is so upset that he breaks the tablets of the Law. These people don't deserve the revelation, one of whose commandments was not to fashion an image of God. And Moses has to plead with God to give them a second chance, reminding God that they had been raised in Egypt where representations of the gods were all around.

About twelve hundred years after that, there was another case of people feeling the need to see God in order to believe that God was real and that God cared. When I was about eleven, I asked my Hebrew teacher at the Brooklyn Jewish Center "If our religion is true, how come there are so many more Christians in the world than Jews?" He answered, "Because it's a lot easier to be a Christian. You don't have to keep kosher, you don't have to keep Shabbos, you don't have to eat matzo on Pesach. And people like to take the easy way." Only years later did I realize what a bad answer that was.

First, I think it's a mistake to describe Judaism primarily in terms of how hard it is, how much you have to give up. Secondly, I'm not sure that when it comes to religion, people want to take the easy way. Often people are attracted by a religion that takes itself seriously enough to make demands on them. But mostly, I can appreciate that, as an Orthodox Jew, he didn't understand the appeal of Christianity. He could only see it in Jewish terms. As I see it, Christianity is spiritually attractive to a lot of people precisely because it lets you see God. Christianity began at a time of great turmoil, a time when hope and faith were in short supply. Like the Jews enslaved in Egypt, people of the first century suffered the cruelties of the Roman Empire at its worst. It was hard for them to believe that God was anywhere in their world. So Christianity offered to show them God in human form. You're not sure that God exists? Here is God come down to earth in the form of this young man. You want to know what this God looks like that you're praying to? Here's what He looks like.

The trouble is, that approach solves some problems but raises others. I once heard a lecture by a Roman Catholic nun who was a psychotherapist, about the spiritual problems of religious women. One thing she said was that, if you picture God as a man, as Christianity does, it becomes nearly impossible for a woman to pray without bringing into her prayer life all the baggage of her relationships with powerful men. Trying to pray, she will be suspicious, flirtatious, resentful, anything but reverent. Picture if you will a fifty-year-old man, a Roman Catholic computer programmer, who has just lost his job. His company has let him go and replaced him with a thirty-year-old Jewish man, wearing jeans and sporting a beard, who can do his job better and cheaper. The man is distraught. How will he pay his bills? How will he send his kids to college? On the way home, he stops off at his church looking for solace. He tries to pray, looks up at the altar and there he sees God portrayed as a thirty year old Jewish man with a beard. How can he believe that God is on his side?

So, if God is not a thing, if God has no form or shape, not male or female, not young or old, not white or black or yellow, how can we see God? And if we can't see God, how can we know that God is real? Right after the incident of the Golden Calf, Moses confronts God with that problem. He says to God, in effect: I've got a bunch of people down there who are having trouble believing that You are real because they can't see You and they don't know how to believe in something they can't see. If it would prevent future Golden Calf incidents, could we just have a tiny peek at what You look like?

God answers, "You don't get it. The reason you can't see Me is not that I'm hiding, and it's not that you're obtuse. You can't see Me because I have no form or shape. I'm not a thing." But then, rather than send Moses away empty-handed, God utters what may be the strangest, most puzzling verse in the entire Torah. He says, "Wait here in this cave while I pass by, and then look. You won't be able to see My face, but you'll see My back."

How can that be? God has just insisted that He has no form or shape. God has just severely punished the Israelites for portraying Him in physical form. And now He tells Moses "You can see My back!" Let me suggest that what it means is this: we can't see God but we can see God's after-effects. That's what the reference to seeing His back implies. All we can see of God is the difference that God makes as He passes through our lives, just as you can't see wind; you can only see things being blown around by the wind. Hagar didn't see God. She saw a well that saved her life. She found the world sustaining her when everyone else had rejected her, and that was enough to persuade her that God was real. Abraham didn't see anything on that mountaintop. He got the message that it was wrong to sacrifice his child on the altar of his beliefs, and he understood, the way a person will say, "Oh, now I see", - he understood what it meant to follow God's ways. And the Israelites in Egypt didn't see God either. They saw God's impact. They saw the gates of freedom swing open, and they knew that God was at work.

In a way, we ought to be able to understand this concept better than previous generations could, because of advances that have been made in subatomic particle physics. No scientist has ever seen an electron. No physicist has ever actually seen a quark. But they are absolutely convinced that quarks and electrons exist, because when they look through their microscopes, they see things happening that could only happen if quarks and electrons were real. And that's what I'm saying, and that's what the Torah is saying, about God. You and I can't see God, but we see things happening that could only be happening because God is at work.

When a doctor saves a life through surgery or cures an illness with antibiotics, he is entitled to feel that he has seen the hand of God at work. When a person is ashamed of herself for something she has done and is afraid that people will shun her but she discovers that there is forgiveness in the world, or when she finds the power within herself to love people close to her who have disappointed her, she can feel that she has met God in her life, not God's face but God's back. Working invisibly, imperceptibly, God has made something happen, because forgiveness doesn't come naturally to people. We can forgive and we can love only when God stirs our souls. When a person finds himself alone, through bereavement or through rejection, and feels utterly abandoned, the way Hagar did in the desert, and friends rally to his or her side, that is God in action, God making things happen.

Some of you may remember that several years ago I went to Oklahoma City to conduct a workshop for clergy and psychologists who were dealing with families who had lost loved ones in the bombing of the Federal Building. After the workshop, I met the bereaved families. I said to them, "It's been a month since that tragedy. What one thing more than anything else has helped you deal with your loss?" And remarkably they all gave me the same answer, using the same word: community. Neighbors, strangers coming up to them to hug them, to express sympathy, to bring them food to fill the emptiness inside them. And I realized that they were giving me a profoundly religious answer. A 19th Century Hassidic rabbi, Menahem Mendel of Rymanov, once said "human beings are God's language." That is, when you cry out to God, God responds to your cry by sending you people. I would paraphrase that sentence to say that human beings, reaching out to others in need, doing good things when they don't have to do them, are as close as we will ever come to seeing the face of God. And it happens all the time.

Any time we find ourselves stirred to be more generous, more courageous, more self-disciplined, more grateful, we may not have seen God face-to-face but we will have caught a glimpse of God's back and seen the difference God can make in our lives.

Any time a Jew does something that calls for a blessing, we are asserting that God is present. Can you see the difference between saying "Praised are You O Lord our God who brings forth food from the earth" and saying "Praised is God who brings forth food from the earth"? To say "You" in a prayer is to claim that God is there with you. God is not in the place; God is in the moment, in the spark of gratitude for food expressed in a Jewish religious idiom. When you light the Shabbat candles, when you say Kiddush over the wine, and you say *"Barukh Attah Adonai"*, you are recognizing the invisible presence of God in your home at that moment. You are saying, I am doing this because God is real and God is stirring me. God is teaching me to create a moment of holiness.

Three thousand years ago, a band of Israelites yearned to see God so desperately that they fashioned a Golden Calf and told themselves "That's what God looks like." And God got very upset with them and said to them "You don't get it. I'm not an object. I'm not a thing you can draw a picture of, or make a statue of. I am the Power that liberated you and guided you for the last few months and will continue to liberate and guide you, even if you can't see Me as I do it."

Two thousand years ago, some people felt they needed to see God, so they came to believe that a young Jew from Nazareth was God in human form. And God said, "No, I'm not incarnate in one person any more than I am incarnate in every person, young and old, black and white, male and female, plain and attractive. They are all My image."

And we today yearn to see God. We come to services on Rosh HaShanah and we virtually challenge God: Reveal Yourself! Make something happen so I'll know that You're there. And God says to us, "Forget about it. You're not going to see Me. Nobody can see Me. I'm not a person and I'm not a thing. I'm not a calf and I'm not a carpenter's son. You want to see Me? Go out and do godly things. Help the poor and comfort the grieving. Make your community a better place, and then go home and look in the mirror. That's as close as you will come to seeing what God looks like. Watch the things you say and control you behavior, and you will feel Me as a living presence in your life. Write a check to tzedakah and you will feel God guiding your hand as you sign it. Light the Shabbat candles, make your table an altar and your home a sanctuary, and you will feel My presence so strongly that you will say, *"Barukh Attah Adonai Eloheynu Melekh HaOlam Asher Kidshanu B'mitzvotav..."* Praised are You, O Lord, who by Your presence has shown me how to bring holiness into my home and into my life."

A WIND SO GREAT it could destroy the
world –I take that as a symbol of a despair
so deep, so stifling that if everybody got
sucked into it, all life would end. It would
be an emotional black hole. Nobody would
have the energy to go on living. That is what
happened to Job when his family died. He
could no longer believe in God. That is what
happened to Jonah when God asked him to
preach to the wicked people of Nineveh.
He gave up on humanity.

In Search of Lost Faith

Yom Kippur 1993

Last December, Suzette and I were in Israel for a family wedding, and we had the opportunity to tour the excavations being done around the South Wall of the ancient temple. You are probably familiar with the Western Wall, the Kotel, once called the Wailing Wall, which was believed to be all that remained of the Second Temple that was destroyed by the Romans nineteen hundred years ago. But unless you've been back to Jerusalem recently, you many not know that archaeologists have discovered almost the entire southern wall of the Temple, including remnants of the actual steps people went up to enter the Temple precincts.

I was remembering our tour of those archaeological sites when I ran across this passage in the Talmud: People coming to pray at the Temple would enter through the right gate, bring their offerings, and then leave through the left exit. That is, they would go counterclockwise. But mourners, those seriously ill, and people seeking a lost object would do the opposite. They would enter through the left gate, travel clockwise, and exit through the right side.

Did you respond to that passage as I did? What is the lost object doing in there? I can understand having a separate category for people who are in mourning or are desperately ill. It's understandable that they would feel out of sync with worshippers who are coming to the Temple to celebrate something. But why put the person who has lost something in the same category?

I can think of two possible answers. One is the feeling we all have when you're looking for something and can't locate it. You're sure you put the car keys right there a few minutes ago and now you're running late and you can't find them. Or that piece of paper with the important phone number on it. You know where you left it but it's not there now. And that can drive a person crazy and make him unfit company for anybody. That's one possible explanation.

The second possibility is that the lost object the passage speaks of isn't just any lost object, your glasses or your keys, but refers to something specific, to *a person who has lost his or her faith* and comes to the Temple hoping to find it there. I sense that every year when we gather here for the High Holy Days. We come to synagogue in a festive mood. We wear our nicest clothes, we have family and friends around us, we look forward to the service, to the familiar melodies, to the sounding of the shofar. There is an air of celebration as we begin the New Year together.

But every year, there are some people among us who are coming from a totally different direction. Some of them have come from the doctor's office, and when the rest of the congregation is chanting *B'rosh HaShanah yikatevun*, "It is decided on Rosh HaShanah and confirmed on Yom Kippur, who shall live and who shall die, who shall prosper and who shall suffer," they hear those words differently from the rest of us. They sit here wondering if *they* are going to be inscribed one more time in the Book of Life, or whether they are hearing those words for the last time.

For some members of the congregation, what they see around them on Yom Kippur is not every seat filled. They see that empty seat where someone they loved used to sit and share those services with them, and that person isn't there any more. They see their neighbors arriving as couples, as families, and like the mourners in ancient Jerusalem, they feel out of step with the worshippers around them.

And then there are those of us who fit into the third category, men and women coming to the Temple in search of a lost object, in search of the faith they might have had as a child and lost somewhere along the way. They see their neighbors familiar with the Hebrew prayers, enthusiastically joining in the chants, and they ask themselves, "What are they feeling that I can't feel?" They think of all the devoutly religious people they know, Jewish and gentile, and wish they had a little of their certainty, their serenity.

In ancient Jerusalem, people like that had their own special entrance to the Temple. They were asked to go the wrong way on a one-way street, entering by the door through which everyone else was coming out. I suspect this was done, not to embarrass them or to isolate them, not to keep them away from the other worshippers. I suspect it was done to *heal* them, so that somehow the other worshippers coming out of the Temple would comfort the mourners, would give hope to the suffering and would restore faith to those who had lost their faith.

On Yom Kippur afternoon, with about three hours to go in our 24-hour fast, we read the story of Jonah, the reluctant prophet. God commands Jonah to go to the distant city of Nineveh in far-off Assyria, and call on the people there to repent. Jonah doesn't want to. He doesn't want to save the Ninevites. He doesn't think they deserve it. So he gets on a ship going in the other direction. A great storm comes up and threatens to destroy the ship. Jonah is thrown overboard, swallowed by a large fish, and the story goes on from there.

But a rabbinic comment on that story reads, "Three times in the Bible we read of a wind so strong that it threatens to destroy the world: in the story of Jonah; in the story of Job where a massive windstorm destroys his home with his family in it; and in the story of Elijah who runs away from Israel because it has become so filled with idol worship and runs back to Mount Sinai where God appears to him in a great wind."

A wind so great that it threatens to destroy the world. I take that as a symbol of a despair so deep, so stifling that if everybody got sucked into it, all life would end. It would be an emotional black hole. No one would have the energy to go on living. That's what happened to Job when his children died. He could no longer believe in God. Life lost all meaning. That's what happened to Jonah when God asked him to preach to the wicked people of Nineveh. Jonah gave up on humanity. He couldn't convince himself that they were capable of becoming any better than they were. And that's what happened to Elijah. He gave up on the Jewish people. And according to the Talmud, the cure for all of them was to go in the door that everyone else was coming out of.

The answer to Job, who lost his faith in God when he saw people around him suffer and die, was not theology but people, not explanation but consolation. As one Hassidic rabbi put it, "human beings are God's language." When you cry out to God, "how can You let things like this happen?" God answers you by sending you people, people to work day and night to try to make you whole, people to sit with you and cry with you and assure you that you are not alone and not rejected, people to bear witness that they once stood where you are standing. And it was hard, but they survived and you'll survive too. That's what you do with tragedy: you don't explain it, you don't try to justify it. You survive it.

I've seen that happen. I've seen it happen in my life; I've seen it happen in the lives of so many of you. You're hurt, you're bereaved, you're angry. You come to shul for the minyan and you see three or four other people there, mourners who are there to say Kaddish even as you are, and you feel less alone, less singled out by cruel fate. You come to shul and you find half a dozen of your neighbors who have gotten up an hour early or have taken an hour out of their evening schedule to make sure you have a minyan, and you are touched and strengthened by that. You know, you can say 98% of the prayers in the siddur at home by yourself. You don't need a minyan. But a few prayers that have to do with experiencing God's holiness, like the Mourners' Kaddish, can only be said with a minyan because when you are depressed and hurt and confused, it's hard to find God by yourself. It's easier to find God in the incarnation of people who gather around you because they want to help. People reach out to you, people show that they care, and in doing so they wash away that sense of rejection. There is holiness in that.

I was in St. Louis recently, speaking to five thousand people who had come together to clean up the small towns of Missouri that had been ravaged by a flood. The question on everyone's mind was "how could God let this happen?" And the answer to that question was not theology. The answer was five thousand people coming together to sweep away the mud and restore the homes and stores. That's what gave people their faith back.

I was in Miami last October, after Hurricane Andrew, celebrating Simchat Torah in a synagogue that had been badly damaged by the storm. Services were held in a classroom that had been spared the damage, and for Kiddush afterward we could have used the main sanctuary as a sukkah because you could look up and see the sky through the damaged roof. But for that Miami congregation, the hurricane was not an act of God. It was an act of nature. The act of God was the willingness of people to rebuild their homes, to rebuild their synagogue, to rebuild their lives after the storm.

That is why, when the tornado demolished Job's home and destroyed his family and blew away his faith in the world as a livable place, his prescription was to go to the Temple and enter through the left door, so that all of the people coming the other way could stop for a moment and offer him a word of condolence, could hug him and comfort him and witness to him that they too had suffered and survived, and so would he.

God's promise is not that everything will be all right. God's promise is that, when things are not all right, you'll be all right because He will be with you. He will be with you in the incarnation of good friends and good people who will give you back your faith.

Jonah didn't lose his faith in God. He lost his faith in humanity. Jonah had no problems believing in God. It was people he couldn't believe in. They weren't worth saving because if they were to be given another chance, they would just go back and repeat their mistakes over again. Jonah didn't want to preach to the people of Nineveh not because they were distant but because they were Assyrians. They were Israel's enemies, they had done terrible things to his people and he didn't believe they were capable of doing better. In effect, Jonah said to God, "I know those people aren't going to change for the better because I know myself. I'm a much nicer person than any of them and I know how hard it is for me to shed bad habits and develop good ones." That is why, when God tells him to go to Nineveh, he answers "What's the point? What difference will it possibly make? Human nature is human nature."

But God says to him, "Look, I know human nature at least as well as you do. You only see the headlines; I see the hearts behind the headlines. You read of the crime; I see the hundreds of people who grieve, who protest, who speak out. You read about the child who disappeared and the police suspect foul play. I see the hundreds of people who give of their time and strength to search for her. You see so many examples of greed and fraud and I see all the people who open their hearts and their pocketbooks for worthy causes."

"More than that," God goes on to say, "You only see people in one dimension of time, where they are today. I can see them in three dimensions. I see where they started, where they are now, and where they are capable of ending up. I see the potential for growth and change, while you over the short span of one life see only the recurring problem. I can see where things that were once tolerated in war, in society, in families, are now no longer acceptable. I have seen people be embarrassed by some of their habits. I have seen them grow and change for the better. And before you leave Nineveh, you will see that too."

That is why people like Jonah, people who have lost their faith in humanity, are told to go to the Temple and go in a different door from anyone else. Don't see people on their way in to the service, when they are a lot like you, burdened by doubts and overwhelmed by a sense of their own shortcomings. Meet them rather on the way out, after the encounter with God has had a chance to work its magic on them.

One of the offerings that people would bring to the Temple in ancient days was the *korban hattat,* the sin offering brought by the person who had done something he or she was ashamed of. I think in some ways, fasting on Yom Kippur is the modern equivalent of the sin offering. People brought it, not to bribe God to deal mercifully with them and not to try to balance the books by doing something good to make up for whatever bad thing they had done. They brought it to acquaint themselves with their better nature, their more generous side. They brought it in the same spirit that people give to charity or come to synagogue today, so that they could say to themselves, "Sometimes I'm petty and narrow-minded, but sometimes I'm capable of being good and kind and generous." The Talmud tells us "there was no happier person in all of Jerusalem than the person who brought his sin offering and left feeling forgiven." That's why the rule calls for the man who doubts whether human beings can ever grow and change and improve to go through the left door, to meet people on the way out, people who feel cleansed, who feel forgiven, who feel better about themselves, and let those people teach him something about what human beings are capable of.

The case of Elijah and his loss of faith is an interesting one, and in some ways the most relevant today. Elijah lost faith in the Jewish people. He saw them becoming ordinary, like everybody else. He saw them put idols in their living rooms like their Canaanite neighbors. According to the narrative in the Book of Kings, he ran away in despair, all the way back to Mt. Sinai where the Jewish adventure as

God's people began. And there he called out to God, to the God who had revealed Himself to Israel and given them the Torah. He said, "You entered into a covenant with this people and they have forsaken Your covenant. They refuse to be a special people. They worship gods of nature, of impulse, even as the pagans do. They chase after material success and trample Your values in the process."

We then read that God responds to Elijah not in thunder, not in a whirlwind, but in a still small voice. We are never told exactly what God says to him, so Jewish tradition fills in the blanks. There are two occasions when the prophet Elijah is welcomed into our homes, when we set a place for him as an honored guest. Do you remember what they are? One is the Pesach seder; we pour a cup of wine for Elijah and open the door to welcome him. The second is at the bris of a baby boy. The chair on which the *sandek* sits to hold the baby is called "the throne of Elijah" and the opening words of the ceremony invoke his presence.

Why Elijah and why those two occasions? The usual answer is that Elijah is supposed to be the herald of the Messiah, the messenger who will come to tell us that the messianic era is at hand. So every Pesach, on the anniversary of our liberation from Egyptian slavery, we say "maybe this will be the year that will see all people free." And whenever a Jewish boy is born, we think to ourselves "maybe he will be the one."

But the tradition gives a second interpretation as well. It sees God offended on our behalf when Elijah says, "Look at those people; they have forsaken Your covenant." So God compels Elijah to attend every bris, that he might see how Jewish families are still passing on the covenant from generation to generation. And God sends him to visit every home where a seder is taking place, that he might get the message "these are My people. They may not do everything I tell them to. They may not do very much of what I tell them to. But at crucial moments in their lives, they cannot forget that they are Jews."

It is easy today to be discouraged about the future of the American Jewish community, the low levels of observance and the high levels of assimilation. But if we let ourselves lose faith in the Jewish people as Elijah did, that despair can be a wind that threatens to destroy the world. It's hard to believe that we can once again be a vibrant, committed Jewish community, but it's dangerous to believe that we can't. We have to do what God told Elijah to do, to stop looking only at what people are doing wrong and look at what continues to remind them that they are Jewish.

There is a joke that was old when I was a child, about the man crawling on his hands and knees around a lamppost, looking for something. A friend comes by and asks him what he is doing, and he replies, "I dropped my keys and I can't find them." The friend asks, "Did you drop them here under the lamppost?" The man answers, "No, I dropped them down the block, but I'm looking here because the light is better."

If you are looking for a lost physical object, you won't find it unless you look where you lost it. But if you are looking for something spiritual, if you are looking for your lost faith, maybe it does make sense to look where there is more light, even as in ancient Jerusalem, people whose faith had been shattered by a mighty wind went looking for it in the Temple. There they met other people who had suffered and who had found God in their ability to survive the worst that fate could deal them. There they met people who had been mean and petty and selfish and disliked themselves for it, but had grown and changed and had found God in their ability to grow and change. And there they met Jews who didn't think very often about their Jewishness but when they did, they found it cleansing and calming, full of light and full of hope. Walking into the Temple by the left-hand door, they met people walking out saying "You know, we really ought to do this more often." And when they met them, and when they saw and heard what the life-giving contact with the Temple had done for them, that which had been lost was found.

God gave Sarah something precious,

but it wasn't hers to keep forever.

It was her responsibility

to take good care of it even though

one day she would have

to relinquish it.

Given On Loan

Yom Kippur 2003

Yom Kippur, the Day of Atonement, brings to a close the High Holy Day season with which the New Year starts, ten days that ask us to look at ourselves, to look at our lives, and to look into our Jewish tradition to find and select the values that we want to guide our lives in the coming year.

Today I would like to go back to the opening moments of Rosh HaShanah, to the first words of the first Torah reading on the first day of a New Year. As many of you will remember, it is the story of the birth of Isaac to Abraham and Sarah after many years of longing. It begins *va'Adonai pakad et Sarah ka'asher amar*, "The Lord took note of Sarah as He had promised to," and to her great joy, she gives birth to a child. At least that's what the translation says it says, but that's not what the Hebrew verb *pakad* usually means. I looked it up in my Bible dictionary and found seven definitions. It most often means "to punish." It can also mean "to command, to organize, to arrange, to appoint or designate." The dictionary lists only one instance where it may mean to remember, to take note, and it's the one I cited from the Rosh HaShanah reading. Nowhere else in the Bible does it mean that.

And then there is one other sense in which *pakad* is sometimes used. I don't think it's what the Bible had in mind in the passage I quoted, but one of the wonderful things about Biblical Hebrew, and one of the things that makes it so hard to appreciate in translation, is that the same word can mean several different things at the same time, and the poor translator has to settle on one and exclude the others.

When I was fourteen and I opened a gemara for the first time in my life and I looked at my first page of Talmud, the very first passage I was taught began *Hamafkid etzel havero*, If you give something to a friend to take care of for you, what is the extent of the friend's responsibility if something happens to it? The Talmud goes on to consider the circumstances: why did you give it to him? Is he doing you a favor by taking care of it? Are you paying him to care for it, in which case his responsibility is greater? Did he ask you to borrow it for his own benefit? Did you alert him to how important it was to you? You see why people who studied Talmud when they were young have an unfair advantage over their classmates when they go to law school.

But for me, the interesting part of that discussion is that the verb for giving someone something temporarily, *mafkid*, is related to the verb from the Rosh HaShanah Torah reading, *pakad*. *Adonai pakad et Sarah ka'asher amar*, God gave Sarah something precious but it wasn't hers to keep forever. It was her responsibility to take good care of it even though one day she would have to relinquish it.

Even if the liturgy of Yizkor on Yom Kippur didn't tell us to do it, we would come to shul on these High Holy Days haunted by memories of people who once shared these services with us and are no longer here to do so. The seats around us are full but we sit here thinking about the empty seats next to us and the people who used to sit in them. It's hard not to feel sad, not to feel somehow diminished, maybe even to feel bitter, to ask "Why? Why couldn't they have remained in our lives longer?" And maybe the answer is hinted at in those first words of the Torah for this season: God sent those people into our lives but they weren't ours to keep forever. They were ours to cherish, to enjoy, to learn from and to love, and one day to be parted from.

To love someone is to make yourself a hostage to fortune. It is to make yourself vulnerable to being hurt in so many ways: by that person's behavior, by that person's shortcomings, by that person's poor judgment, and ultimately by that person's leaving you, whether by choice or by circumstance. And maybe that is why, at this season which is so heavy with memories, which is so laden with prayers for a year of life, which reminds us (as if we needed to be reminded) of all the things that might happen to us and to the people around us in the coming year, — maybe that's why the Rabbis ordained that we begin with those particular words of Torah: *Adonai pakad et Sarah*, God gave Sarah a precious gift and as He did so, He warned her that it would not be hers forever. God said to her, "I have made your soul in such a way that you are capable of connecting with another person, with another soul, husbands and wives, parents and children, brothers and sisters, even friends." One of the most beautiful verses in the entire Bible describes what David and Jonathan felt for each other as best friends: "And David's soul was intertwined with the soul of Jonathan." And God goes on to say to Sarah and to every one of us: "When you have that in your life, cherish it because it is so special and cherish it because it won't last forever."

The poet Wallace Stevens has written "Death is the mother of beauty." I understand that to mean that we appreciate the beautiful things in our lives precisely because they are so fragile, because they won't last forever. We appreciate the beauty of a New England autumn because it is only here for a short time, the leaves dying and going out in a blaze of red and yellow and orange. If they looked like that all year round, who would bother to drive up to Vermont to see them? *Adonai pakad et Sarah*, God gave Sarah something precious and told her not to waste any time, to love it promptly and unceasingly because it would not be hers forever.

It's not only death that separates us from the precious gifts that God has sent into our lives. Time can do it as well. Parents grow old and needy and forgetful, and can no longer be the forceful presence in our lives that they once were, and we feel that we have lost something. Friends grow distant with time. Children grow up and no longer greet us with hugs when we come home. I can imagine God saying to Sarah, "You've been praying for a child for all these years. Do you really know what you're letting yourself in for? You know the pain of being childless, and it is a very real pain. But you're about to find out how painful it can be to be a parent."

When God curses Eve after the incident of the forbidden fruit in the Garden of Eden, telling her "in great pain will you bear children," the careful reader notices that the Bible uses the same word for "great pain" that it uses a few pages later when it speaks of how much it pained God to see how human beings were behaving in the time of Noah, as if God were saying "I know what it feels like to see people you care about doing bad things and to see other people you love suffering and not be able to stop the misbehavior or relieve the suffering."

But Sarah persists, so God send her a child. But God says to her, "Let's make one thing clear at the outset. He's yours to raise, he's yours to nurture, but he's not yours to keep forever."

I would remind you of those famous lines from Kahlil Gibran in *The Prophet*:

> "Your children are not your children;
> they are the sons and daughters
> of life's longing for itself...
> You may give them your love but not your
> thoughts, for they have their own thoughts...
> You are the bows from which your children
> as living arrows are sent forth."

Children grow up, children grow distant. Nature compels them to declare their independence from us, to prove that they have minds and lives of their own. And sometimes during those difficult years we may feel that we are losing them. That is when we have to remember God's words to Sarah: we can't lose them, any more than we permanently lose parents and other loved ones to death. We can't lose them first because they were ours to give life to and to raise but they were never ours to keep. And we can't lose them because the tie between a parent and a child is too intimate to be left behind entirely.

That's why I advocate the Little Bo Peep theory of relating to grown children: leave them alone and they'll come home. Try to own them and they will do their best to throw off the chains and escape. But maintain a loving, caring relationship with them even if it's not easy, and maybe when they turn thirty and have children of their own, they'll feel pleased rather than cursed when they realize they're turning into you. And maybe then they'll find their way back home of their own free will. You may remember visiting a son or daughter in their college dorm rooms and finding a poster on their wall with a quotation from <u>Jonathan Livingston Seagull</u> that reads, "If you love something, let it go. If it comes back to you, it will be yours forever. If it doesn't, it was never really yours."

To find someone you can love, to find someone your soul truly connects with, is a precious gift, made even more precious when we realize how fragile it is. Elizabeth Kubler-Ross in her autobiography writes of having had a really good friend, someone she felt closer to than she did to her family. They were soul mates, sharing their most intimate dreams and feelings.

Then one day something happened. Dr. Kubler-Ross was facing a crisis. She turned to her friend for emotional support and for whatever reason, the friend wasn't there for her. Kubler-Ross was more than hurt; she felt betrayed. The relationship was never the same after that. They drifted apart, stopped calling each other, lost touch. Then one day a year or so later, she ran into the friend, who seemed genuinely pleased to see her. No guilt, no embarrassment. The former friend insisted they have lunch together. Their lunch conversation was almost entirely about catching up with each other's families.

If Kubler-Ross anticipated an explanation or an apology, none was offered. Leaving the restaurant, Kubler-Ross realized she couldn't be angry with her former friend any more. There was no rejection, no betrayal. What there was was the realization that there had once been something very meaningful between them and it wasn't there any more. Its time had passed. A friendship, like any other living thing, can flourish for a while and then it dies. Kubler-Ross realized that, rather than being angry at its loss, the right thing for her to do was to be grateful for all that it had added to her life while she had it. Rather than think of herself as poorer for no longer having that relationship, she should realize how much richer she was for once having had it.

It reminded me of the painful column that Ann Landers had to write some years ago, telling her millions of readers that her marriage was ending. She rejected the implication that she, who told others how to handle their marital problems, had been unable to handle her own. She said instead that there were no victims and no villains in this story. There was only a beautiful relationship that nourished her for many years but couldn't make it to the finish line.

Over the years, I've spoken to many of you when your marriages were in difficulty. I know how hard it is not to feel angry and not to feel that you have somehow failed. And I was always struck by the terrible sadness I would feel in discovering how years of love, years of sharing and caring, could be washed away by the rancor that attends a marital breakdown. What happened to all that love, all those intimate memories? Where do they go? How does something like that just disappear? And maybe the healthiest response to the end of a marriage would be like our response to the end of a life, to the death of a parent, even of a child, to say to ourselves as Ann Landers did: I had something very beautiful for a while and it added so much to my life while it was there. I remember how happy I was back then. But it just wasn't meant to last.

I'm not asking those of you in that situation to deny your pain or your anger, any more than I would ask you to deny it at a funeral. What I'm asking, in the name of sparing yourself the bitterness, the self-blame and the self-definition of yourself as a rejected victim, is that you not let the unhappy, acrimonious ending utterly obliterate the memory of the happiness you once had. You're deprived of so much when a marriage goes bad. You're deprived of so much when someone you love dies slowly and painfully until you find yourself wishing it would end already. Why should you be deprived of those good memories as well?

There are other gifts that God gives us, to cherish while we have them because they won't be ours forever. With every passing year, with every turn of the page of the calendar to a New Year, our bodies and our minds grow older and at a certain point, you realize you can't do things you used to be able to do. We can make jokes about senior moments (I heard a really good one the other day...but I can't remember it), but like jokes about sex, money and relatives, it's just another instance of our using humor to pretend that something that makes us anxious doesn't make us anxious.

How do those of us on the downhill side of life respond to being a year older? We can lament, we can grieve for the loss of mental acuity and bodily vigor. We can be jealous of younger people who still have what we've begun to lose. Or we can bask in the glow of the memories of who we once were because those memories can't be taken away from us. Every passing year leaves us with more past, more memories than we had before. And we can take stock of what we have acquired to compensate for what we may have lost. If we could get over seeing life as something that gets used up year by year and learn to see life as the accumulation of wisdom, if we could remind ourselves that in today's world wisdom is more of an enduring gift than muscle power, then we will have less reason to fear growing old.

So we come to shul on Yom Kippur and we say to God, "Why do You tease us like this, God? Why do you send these beautiful people into our lives and then take them away when we need them most? Why can't they last forever?" And God says, "I can't do that. I can't cure a sick person every time somebody prays for him. I can't postpone death indefinitely because someone is loved. If I did that, pretty soon there would be no room in the world for young families to have babies. That's why I tried to warn Abraham and Sarah that this precious gift I was giving them was theirs to love and to enjoy but not to keep forever. But if I can't give you the gift you keep asking for, the gift of eternity, I have two other gifts for you to make up for it. I've given you the gift of memory and the capacity for gratitude."

As many of you know, I have a new book out, a meditation of the 23rd Psalm. I describe it as a drama in three acts. In act one, the author's life is serene and placid, — still waters and green pastures. Then in act two, he finds himself in the valley of the shadow, his life disrupted by sorrow and loss. And it is there that he discovers what God is really about, not the God of happy endings but the God who takes you by the hand and leads you through the valley of the shadow so that you don't have to spend the rest of your life in darkness. Act three is a hymn of praise to the God whom he has come to know and feel close to. The line "my cup runneth over," the line about how grateful he is for all the blessings in his life, comes *after* the part about being in the valley of the shadow of death. Under the immediate impact of what happened to him, he can only think about what he has lost. But given time and some perspective, he is able to focus on what he had and what in a sense he still has.

There is a prayer in our Mahzor by Rabbi Morris Adler - sometimes we read it at the Yizkor service - that says in part:

"Shall I cry out in anger, O Lord, because Your gifts
are mine but for a while?

Shall I forget the blessing of health the moment it
gives way to illness and pain?
Shall I grieve for a youth that has gone once my hair
is gray and my shoulders bent, and forget the days
of vibrancy and power?
Shall the time of darkness put out forever the glow
of the light in which once I walked?"

So here we are on a day when we bring so many poignant memories to shul with us, and we say to God, "Why does it have to hurt so much?" And God answers "If you didn't have the memories, painful as they may be, you would have lost those people, you would have lost those good years, those transcendent moments forever. Then you would really have lost them."

And the Lord said to Sarah "Here is something precious, something beautiful to enrich and brighten and complicate your life and fill it with meaning. It's yours to cherish, it's yours to care for. It's just not yours forever, although once you have loved it, it will be yours forever. Do you still want it on those terms?"

The Lord gives but the Lord does not take away. He teaches us to fill the empty spaces in our lives with memories of what once we had and with gratitude for what we still have, and our cup runneth over.

IF SOMEBODY HURTS YOU or

offends you, you are entitled to be upset

with him for a couple of days. If you

persist in being angry into the third day,

you are keeping a grievance on life support

that would otherwise have died of natural

causes after forty-eight hours.

FORGIVENESS

Yom Kippur 1984

I knew a man when I was young — he was a friend of my parents, — who was a kind of Jew you virtually can't find any more. He was a Bundist, a Yiddishist-Socialist. He loved the Jewish people, Jewish culture, Jewish ethics, with a passion, but he had no patience for Jewish religion. At the time, I could never understand why he would fast on Tisha B'Av and eat on Yom Kippur, until one day he explained it to me. "Tisha B'Av", he said, "is about Jewish suffering, about how hard it is to be a Jew in the Diaspora. That means a lot to me. I care about Jewish suffering. But Yom Kippur, what is that all about? About sin, about repentance, about confessing our sins to God. What do I care about things like that?"

I was a youngster at the time and I wasn't about to get into an argument with him about how he wanted to express his Jewishness. It was only many years later that I understood that Yom Kippur is not really about sin and apologizing to God. What this day is really about is one word that ought to be important to us, and which we don't stop and think about often enough, which is why we need a holiday dedicated to it. The word is "Forgiveness." From the opening lines of Kol Nidre and the verses which follow it to the story of Jonah, which we'll read tomorrow afternoon, this whole day is about forgiving and being forgiven. If Yom Kippur is important to us, then the idea of forgiveness ought to be more important to us than it usually is.

We need to hear that, because so many of us have permitted our lives to become constricted by feuds, grudges, decisions we made years ago that we weren't going to speak to someone anymore or let him into our lives, decisions we've kept more faithfully than most promises we make to ourselves. I found myself thinking about forgiveness this summer, because of a passage in the Torah and a call from a graduate student in Wisconsin, and I wanted to share what I was thinking with you tonight.

First, the Torah passage: The legal code of ancient Israel made a distinction between premeditated murder and manslaughter. If you deliberately killed somebody, you were executed in return. But if you caused someone's death accidentally, you still had to suffer the lesser penalty of temporary exile, so that you wouldn't run into the victim's family in the market, but your life was spared. What if you claimed it was an accident but others weren't so sure? The Torah says that if you had been on bad terms with the victim, if you were known to be enemies, then it would be hard for you to claim inadvertence. The precise language reads as follows: *v'hu lo soneh lo mitmol shilshom.* (Deut. 19:4). If he was not your enemy yesterday or the day before, then we accept your claim that it was an accident. "If he was not your enemy yesterday or the day before ..." Commenting on that verse, the Talmud says: This is the definition of an enemy, someone you haven't gotten along with for three days.

Do you understand the implications of that comment? What it says to me is this: if somebody hurts you, offends you, lets you down, you're entitled to be upset with him for a couple of days. These things happen between close friends, casual acquaintances, members of a family. Somebody treats you wrong — it's perfectly all right to be angry with him for a day or two, today and tomorrow. The Torah says you can do that. But by the third day, you ought to be over your anger and be friends with him again. Relationships ought to be able to survive a 24-to-48 hour frost. Now comes the important part: if you persist in your being angry into a third day, it's because you're choosing to prolong the argument. You're deliberately nursing a grudge, keeping a grievance on life support that would otherwise have died of natural causes after 48 hours.

Why would anybody do that? Why would anyone deliberately choose to prolong unpleasantness? I think we know the answer, but it's one of those nasty little secrets we don't like to think about. There is something perversely satisfying about being the injured party. It makes us feel righteous, in some way morally superior. We can look down with scorn on the person who hurt us. We feel nobler being the wounded one rather than being the inflicter of the wound; it gives us the weapon of guilt to use against the other person, and as Leonard Fein has written, "Guilt is to Jews what oil is to Arabs, our major source of energy."

If you believe in a world of morality and not a world of trickery and power, then you would rather be the moral one, the one in the right, than the one who took advantage and inflicted the wrong. If we ever stopped hurting and bleeding, if we ever admitted that the incident was over and done with, we would lose that moral advantage.

Simon Wiesenthal, the Nazi hunter, in the midst of a fairly grim autobiography, tells one wonderful story. There was a man living near him in one of the D. P. camps after the war who borrowed ten dollars from him, and assured him that he had a package coming from a relative any day and would positively pay him back the next week. At week's end, he had an excuse for not paying, and the next week, he had an even better one, and so it went on for almost a year. Finally one day, the man came up to him with a ten-dollar bill in his hand and said, "My visa has just come through. I'm leaving for Canada tomorrow. Here's the ten dollars I owe you." And Wiesenthal waved him away and said, "No, keep it. For ten dollars, it's not worth changing my opinion of you."

He was wrong, of course. It's a bargain to give away a grudge, a resentment for nothing. To get paid for getting rid of that burden is a double bargain. And this brings me to the Wisconsin graduate student. She called me one day, introduced herself as a graduate student in the School of Social Work, and told me she had gotten a foundation grant to do a study of the dynamics of forgiveness as a social process. What happens when a person forgives someone for having hurt him weeks or months or even years ago? How do they come to that decision? And what is the effect on them afterwards? She was calling me because she had read my book and figured I had been in touch with a lot of people who had been badly hurt by life. Had I been able to guide them through the process of forgiving those who had hurt them? She came out to Natick and we talked. I don't know what she gained from the conversation, but I learned a lot from her.

She told me, for example, that among all the people she interviewed, there was a unanimous agreement on one point. When they forgave someone, when they let go of a grievance they had been carrying for some time, there was for every single one of them a physical sense of relief, a feeling of having put down a burden. They didn't realize they were carrying this load of bitterness until it was taken away from them, and suddenly they felt so much lighter and freer. At some level, they had been enjoying the bittersweet moral posture of being the aggrieved victim and had not wanted to give it up, but now suddenly they discovered it felt a whole lot better not to be a victim any more.

There is a story told of two Buddhist monks making a pilgrimage to a shrine in India. As they are traveling, they come to a large mud puddle, and they see an attractive young girl in a beautiful new dress standing by the edge of the puddle, afraid to cross for fear of ruining her dress. One of the monks impulsively picks her up and carries her across the puddle. The second monk is put off by what his friend did, and for the rest of the day it bothers him. He doesn't say much to his friend, answering him in monosyllables. Finally at the day's end, when they stop to cook their dinner, he says to his companion, "You know, it's not right for people like us to get too close to women. They represent a temptation." And his friend turns to him and says, "Are you still carrying that girl? I put her down six hours ago."

We're all carrying burdens of bitter memories and resentments, which serve no purpose except to weigh us down, to make us feel very noble for being so weighed down, and to create barriers between us and other people. And we can't imagine the sense of relief and freedom we will feel when we find the courage to put those burdens down.

The young social worker who came to interview me told me of one other finding that neither of us could totally understand. There is apparently a close connection between the power to punish and the power to forgive. Not actually punishing, but knowing that you could. When you feel weak, helpless, impotent, then resentment and moral superiority are the only weapons you have. But when you know that you can get even with someone if you wanted to, then for some strange reason you can afford to be magnanimous. It's very common, for example, for someone who has been mugged and robbed to say he would get more satisfaction from knowing that his assailant had been caught and punished than he would from getting his money back.

I thought of the Biblical story of Joseph, how when he was seventeen, his brothers had been jealous of him and sold him into slavery. For twenty years, he lived in the anticipation of getting even with them. He could see it in his mind's eye - how he would make them grovel and plead for their lives just as he had done. And in his mind's eye, he enjoyed every minute of it. He endured loneliness and imprisonment looking forward to that scene.

And then finally one day it happened. His dreams of revenge came true. He was Pharaoh's minister of agriculture in Egypt. There was a famine in the Middle East; only Egypt had grain. And his brothers came down to Egypt from Canaan to buy wheat. Now he had them in his power. Before he would sell them wheat, he made them beg and grovel. He played tricks with them, he threatened them with imprisonment. They had to plead with him for their freedom. And something very strange happened to Joseph.

He found he wasn't enjoying it one bit. He who had dreamed of revenge, he who had lived for revenge, found out that now that he was tasting it, it had turned to ashes in his mouth. He couldn't enjoy what was happening. He felt cheap, unworthy. So Joseph breaks down and cries. He reveals his identity to his brothers, hugs and embraces them, and reassures them that he no longer bears any anger toward them. Joseph discovers that he didn't really want to get even with his brothers, he didn't really want to hurt them as they had hurt him. What he really wanted was the power to hurt them. Once he had it, he didn't have to use it. At that point, he could be magnanimous. He could forgive them, and rid himself of the corrosive burden of hating someone and wanting to hurt them, which he had been carrying for twenty years.

We talked about the religious basis for forgiveness, not just what happens but why. If someone has hurt you — a man has been cheated by a business associate he thought was his friend, a woman's husband leaves her for another woman — my interviewer asked me, "on what basis do you ask a person in that situation to forgive?" She told me she had asked that of several clergymen, and the answers she got generally went something like this: "None of us is perfect; we all do selfish, inconsiderate things. As we would like to be forgiven for the things we do, so should *we* forgive others. It's the noble, charitable thing to do. Forgive him; you'll be a better person for it."

I told her my approach would be different. I don't urge people to be noble. I don't say to them that what that person did was no worse than what you and I do. It may very well have been worse. What I say to the victim of fraud or desertion or inconsiderate treatment is this: If that person hurt you, if he did such a terrible thing to you, he doesn't deserve the right to rent that much space in your mind. He doesn't deserve the power to make you a bitter, resentful person, to change your personality for the worse. You want to get even with him? You don't get even by continuing to hurt, by continuing to seethe with rage so that you can't enjoy the life you have. You don't get even with him by becoming like him, selfish, mistrustful, vindictive. You don't get even by continuing to throw lumps of guilt at him, which he usually dodges, and even if you hit him and hurt him with it, you just feel worse for having done it. Get even by letting go, so that he can no longer pull your emotional strings. Scott Fitzgerald said "living well is the best revenge." I would say "becoming whole, outgrowing bitterness and vindictiveness, living serenely is the best revenge."

My friends, I would like to see you end Yom Kippur significantly lighter than you began it, - not because you will have gone a whole day without eating. That's a very temporary change. I'd like to see you walk out of shul tomorrow evening lighter than you began tonight because you will have divested yourselves of the burdens of bearing grudges, resentments, stale and outdated feuds based on misunderstandings that happened years ago, and like everyone else who has given up a grudge, you'll be astonished by the sense that a burden has been lifted from you. You'll never know how weighted down you have been until you let go of it.

There are three things we have to do tonight and tomorrow, and I'm glad we have all day to do them, without worrying about meals, jobs, school or anything else. These three things will take a lot of effort and concentration on our part.

First, we have to give up the anger and resentment we feel toward people who have hurt us or let us down, — not because they didn't do anything so wrong. What they did may have been monstrously wrong, cowardly, selfish, immoral. That's their problem. Not because they deserve to be forgiven; maybe they do, maybe they don't.

I don't even know how to measure that. We have to give up the anger and the resentment because of what it does to *us*, because it burdens and distorts *us,* and it's just not worth it.

There have been times over the years when some of you in the congregation have disappointed me, when I might have expected you to be more sensitive, more responsible, more committed, and when I looked for it, it wasn't there. But I've gotten over it, I've written it off, not because I'm such a *tzaddik*, not because I'm a saint, but very simply because I don't want to be bothered schlepping all those unpleasant memories around with me for the rest of my life. Who needs them? I don't want them to get in the way of our friendship or our Rabbi-congregant relationship.

And conversely, I'm sure there have been times over the years when I've disappointed you, when you would have wanted me to be more available, more responsive, more flexible. And I hope you've gotten rid of those feelings of disappointment and anger too, not because you've decided that I was right and not because you've decided that I couldn't help myself, but simply because it doesn't do you any good to hold on to those memories today.

I was visiting a member of the Temple in the hospital one day. He was scheduled for surgery the next morning, and before I left, I took his hand and said the *mi-sheberach* prayer for him. In the middle of the prayer, the man suddenly started to cry. He told me that, years before, he had had an argument with me over something that had happened at the Temple. Whenever he saw me, which wasn't very often, he remembered that argument, and he assumed that whenever I saw him, I remembered it as well, and he couldn't believe I was saying a prayer for him to get well. I, for the life of me, couldn't remember that incident. Like the Buddhist monk in the story, I had put it down a long time ago, and this poor man had continued to carry it all those years.

The second thing we have to do in the next twenty-four hours is to forgive God for all the unfairness in the world, for the sickness and the accidents and the fact that other people were born luckier and better looking and more talented than we were. It's not fair, and I suspect God knows that. But the whole theme of reconciliation on Yom Kippur is in part our way of saying to God, "You know, I have good reasons to be very upset with You, but I'm not going to let that come between us because I need You. I need to be able to turn to You, to talk to You, to get strength and hope from You, and if I'm mad at You, it would just get in the way."

And finally, the last thing we need to achieve is to walk out of here at sunset tomorrow feeling forgiven, feeling cleansed and purified, ready to start the new year. Have we done things in the past year that disappointed and offended God? I'm sure we have, last year and every year. We're only human. Can God forgive us? I don't doubt it for a moment. Not because we've begged and fasted and suffered, but because the God I believe in is a God of forgiveness. He is not so petty or vindictive as to keep score. He has no vested interest in being angry at us. Every page of the Yom Kippur liturgy tells us that we're much harder on ourselves than God is on us. He wants to let bygones be bygones and to start out fresh, if only we could learn to see ourselves from a God's-eye view.

Have we hurt and offended other people during this past year? Friends, neighbors, family? I suspect most of us have, in one way or another. Will they forgive us? That's hard to say. They're a lot less reliable than God is on that score. But that's their problem more than ours. If they choose to go beyond the Torah's 48-hour statute of limitations on being angry, if they choose to be sullen and resentful, they're the ones who will have to carry the emotional baggage of grudge and grievance. If you feel that you have repented and cast out what you did that was wrong, then you should be able to feel cleansed even if they are still angry at you.

My friends, in the days when the Temple stood in Jerusalem and people worshipped God with animal offerings, one of the species of offering was the *hattat,* the atonement offering. If you had done something wrong and felt bad about it, you brought your *korban hattat* and in the process of bringing it, you came to see yourself in a new light, as a person who was sometimes weak but also sometimes strong, sometimes selfish and mean-spirited but sometimes capable of being generous. And you left feeling better about yourself. In fact, the Talmud says that of all the people leaving the Temple, the happiest were the ones who had just brought their atonement offerings and could walk out feeling cleansed and forgiven.

May we who come here hungering for forgiveness, may we who come here seeking to be taught to forgive and to be forgiven, may we on this Day of Atonement bring as sacrifices to God's altar all our lingering anger, our jealousies and resentments, our ancient grudges and grievances, and as they turn into smoke on God's altar and vanish into the air, may we know the joy of walking out of the Temple feeling cleansed and forgiven. AMEN

THE THINGS WE DO FOR OUR CHILDREN when they are growing up - feeding them, teaching them, nursing them through illnesses, staying up all night the first time they use the car, - do we do those things out of sheer love and kindness, because that is what it means to be a parent? Or do we expect to be paid back with interest for all those loving deeds? Will we one day confront our children with those magic guilt-producing words (you know the ones I mean) After all I've done for you..."

No Strings

Kol Nidre 1978

Last month, I was in New York for a meeting with several rabbinic friends of mine, and because it was September, the talk turned to High Holy Day sermons, and what needed to be talked about this year. One of the rabbis present told this true story:

There was an elderly couple who had been married for many years and had no children. Like Abraham and Sarah in the Bible, they loved each other very much, but they felt this one void in their lives. Then totally unexpectedly, the woman found herself pregnant. She could hardly believe it. She went to a doctor and he confirmed it, but he said that because of her general physical condition and age, the pregnancy would be very dangerous for her. He recommended that she terminate it. The woman went through two days of indescribable anguish, and finally decided to go ahead and try to have the child, despite the risks. At her age, she wasn't afraid of death, and the prospect of leaving a child in the world to continue her life was too much of a miracle for her to give up.

Her doctor didn't like the idea. He confined her to bed for the rest of the pregnancy; he checked her into the hospital at the beginning of the ninth month. Finally, the time came for her to deliver. She gave birth to a son, but the strain on her heart was too much, and a few days afterward she died.

The husband raised the boy. He went to school, graduated from high school, and went off to college. In his second year of college, the father discovered him sharing an apartment with a non-Jewish girlfriend and said, "How can you do this to me?" And the boy answered, "It's my life."

The group of us, all rabbis, who heard the story, began to speculate on how we might fit that very moving story into a High Holy Day sermon. Then one of our number said, "I think the boy in the story was selfish and callous and inconsiderate, but you know what else he was? He was right."

He was right. I might wish he had said it more nicely. I might wish he had been more sensitive to where his elderly father was coming from. But fundamentally, if you look beyond the defensiveness and maybe the hostility in his voice, he was saying two things that he is entitled to say.

He is saying first of all, "I'm taking responsibility for my own life. I am old enough now that you can love me and teach me and worry about me, but you have neither the right nor the need to live my life for me. Nobody is entitled to make someone else's life an extension of his own values and beliefs." And the second thing he is saying to his father is, "If you think I'm making a mistake, tell me about it; explain it to me, try to convince me. But don't try to control me by making me feel guilty, because that's dishonest communication. If you can't talk me out of this without bringing my mother's grave into the conversation, then don't mention it at all."

I know this is a hard message for a lot of us to accept. We're all subject to the mistake of seeing our children not as independent human beings to whom we've given life, but as extensions of ourselves. They become our second chance at going through life, with the advantage of the experience we gained first time around. We are, many of us, tempted to say to our children, "When I was your age, I had to do what my parents wanted. Now you should do what I want, and when you have children, you can make them do what you want" — with the prospect that from now till the days of the Messiah, everybody will be living life by proxy.

We don't want to be told that's wrong. We feel justified in exercising that kind of control. But Yom Kippur would be a sham, a day of just going through the motions, if we only talked about those sins that didn't really bother us but avoided the ones that really mattered.

In the Al Chet, the confessional we recite half a dozen times on Yom Kippur, there were many lines that we could recognize as applying to ourselves — misusing words to hurt or fool people, giving in too easily to temptation — but there is one line that ought to puzzle us: *al chet she-chattanu l'fanecha b'neshech uv'marbit,* for the sin we have committed before You by charging excessive interest. Who does that? How many people in the average congregation are Mafia loan sharks? How many are even bankers, charging *reasonable* interest? Why do we all have to say those words?

Maybe it's talking about something else besides lending money. Maybe it's talking about the things we do for our children when they're growing up — feeding them, teaching them, nursing them through their illnesses, staying up all night the first time they use the car. Do we do those things out of sheer love and kindness, because that's what it means to be a parent? Or do we expect to be paid back with interest for all those loving deeds? Will we one day confront our children with those magic guilt-producing words (You know the words I'm referring to), "after all I've done for you?"

When you love someone honestly, maturely, you love without strings attached. You do it for the joy of giving love to someone you care about because you're a caring person. You don't love to establish a claim of obligation on the other person, to make sure you get loved back. If love is something you give, not something you barter with, then you may be disappointed if the other person turns out to be less loving than you, but you have no right to feel cheated.

I once heard a Rabbi give a sermon in which he quoted the old saying, "Why is it that one mother can take care of six children but six children can't take care of one mother?" And I said to myself, 'That's terrible. He shouldn't be saying that. Nobody has the right to play on people's guilt like that. If you want to give a sermon about one's obligations to his parents, fine, do it. If you want to talk about the dignity of the elderly, talk about it. But stop trying to manipulate people by making them feel guilty, because that's a cheap shot.'

And yet religion so often does that. It tries to get us to do things we may not want to do by playing on our guilt. And that's wrong. It's like a boxer who is losing a fight and in his desperation, starts to cheat and to fight unfairly. It used to be that people would perform the mitzvot freely, voluntarily, even joyously. But once they stopped, religious leaders couldn't *persuade* them to do it, so they turned to guilt. And it proved to be a moral shortcut that, as it usually does, ended up doing more harm than good. No honorable cause is served, and nobody benefits, when people are moved to do something worthwhile by being made to feel guilty. Things meant to be done for love lose all taste when done out of guilt or manipulation.

I think, for example, we tend to misunderstand Yom Kippur very seriously. We tend to think of it as a day in which we confront our guilt, a day in which we're hit in the face with all the things we did wrong last year. In fact, Yom Kippur is supposed to be the opposite. Religion is supposed to be a mechanism for making you feel free, not for making you feel guilty. Yom Kippur is intended to be a day that leaves you feeling strong and clean.

Doesn't that rabbi I quoted earlier understand that the six children he's complaining about have their own children, their own families? Hasn't he seen what I've seen in my pastoral experience — teenagers afraid to bring a friend home because there is an elderly grandparent on the verge of senility in the house; husbands and wives whose marriage relationship is being eroded by an in-law who gives them no peace and no privacy? Has that rabbi forgotten that the same Torah which says, "honor your father and mother" also says "therefore shall a man leave his father and mother and cleave unto his wife and they shall become one."

There is a story in a popular Jewish book of the middle ages about a mother bird walking down the road with three baby birds, when they come to a large puddle. It was too deep for the baby birds to walk across and too wide for them to go around. So the mother bird said to the first baby bird, "If I pick you up and carry you across the puddle, how will you repay me for it?" The baby bird said, "The next puddle we come to, I'll pick you up and carry you across." The mother said, "That's a silly answer. You're too small to carry me across." She asked the same question of the second fledgling, and it answered, "when I'm grown up, I'll carry you across puddles." The mother bird shook her head and said, "Even when you're grown up, I won't need you to get across puddles." Then she turned to the third who answered, "Someday I'll be a mother bird and I'll have babies of my own, and I'll do all the things for them that you've done for me." And that, of course, was the right answer.

We love our children, we give them life and sustain them, not because we expect to be paid back with interest, but because we hope that someday they will have children and they will have learned from us how to be parents, so that the river of life and loving kindness flows forward, not backwards, downstream and not up.

We *have* children, but we don't own them. The first person in the Bible ever to be a parent had trouble understanding that. Eve never had parents of her own, and when she gave birth to her first child, she named him Cain, which means "possession". She said, *kaniti ish et Adonai*, I have acquired a person with God's help. He's mine, he belongs to me. You remember how the story ends: Cain commits a terrible murder and leaves home. He becomes a wanderer, and the parent who said "he belongs to me, I own him" never saw him again.

The easy part of being a parent is the physical part. You bring a child into this world, you cut the cord that attaches him to his mother, and physically, you have two separate human beings. The hard part is cutting the psychological cords, letting a child feel that he is growing up and being loved and sent out into the world with no strings attached, that his future is not mortgaged to a sheaf of IOUs for every bandaged knee and every week's allowance, that he has more to look forward to than "when you're a parent, you can live through your children as I'm living through you."

There are some all-too-common ways in which we unfairly use strings of love and guilt to manipulate our children. There is the parent who says, "your happiness is all I care about. If you're happy, I'm happy." It sounds so innocent; it sounds like every devoted Jewish mother. But look at what it's really saying. First of all, what will you do if your child takes you at your word, believes you, and one day says to you, "what's the matter? I'm doing something you don't approve of, but I'm happy. Why are you so sullen? Why are you depressed?"

Because, you see, when we said that, we weren't telling the truth. We didn't really mean it. We meant the very opposite. We really meant "don't you dare be happy unless you make me happy at the same time." And that's not fair. That's pushing the guilt button to make somebody do what we want him to. Why should we retain that power to pull the strings of someone else's life, to make him stop and go on the basis of what pleases us?

To say, "my happiness depends on you", to say it to a child, to say it to a husband or wife, is to put a terrible weapon into their hands, a weapon that is sometimes more than they can handle safely. They're liable to hurt themselves with it. In fact, they are liable to hurt us, to get back at us, by hurting themselves. They are now in a position to say, even if only subconsciously, "your happiness depends on me? Then anytime I'm angry at you, I know how to get even with you — by dropping out of school, by having an unhappy marriage, by messing up my job. I'll hurt *myself* but *you'll* feel it."

You see, and this is the point we very often forget — when you cut the strings that tie parent and child to each other, you set two people free. Before, both parent and child were bound; now they are both liberated.

Do you recognize the name Gary Hansen? He made headlines last spring. Gary Hansen is the young man in Colorado who is suing his parents for raising him wrong, for malpractice of parenthood. He is saying, in the classic outcry of the immature person, "It's not my fault, you made me like this." I can only hope the judge, if his suit ever comes to trial, will introduce Gary Hansen to the young man whose story I told you earlier, who will tell him "stop blaming your parents. It's your life. You can complain about how your parents raised you, and they can complain about how their parents shaped them into being the kind of parents they are, and so on, back to Adam and Eve. But sooner or later, you're going to have to stop blaming other people, and take responsibility for your own life. You'll have to do it, even if your parents don't want you to, even if they're willing to accept responsibility and go on taking the blame for you. And when you do that, you'll make a lot of people, including yourself, freer and happier."

It used to be the custom, when a child became Bar Mitzvah, for the parents to recite a special prayer, the way we now have them say Shehecheayannu. It went: "*Baruch shep'tarani me-onsho shel zeh*, Praised be God who has released me from responsibility for this child." The parents were saying, "My child isn't a little kid anymore. He's becoming an adolescent. It's going to be harder for me to get him to do what I want him to. If I feel that what he chooses to do reflects on me, if I have unfulfilled dreams and fantasies of how he will make me proud and happy, accomplishing the things I was never able to, I may try too hard to make him do what I want. And if I do that, I may smother him so that he'll never develop a mind and soul of his own.

Or if I do that, I may end up fighting dirty to try and control him as he gets bigger and stronger — using guilt, using threats, developing symptoms every time I lose an argument — and I may provoke him into fighting just as hard and just as deviously against me. But if I can cut the strings, if I can love him with no strings attached, if we both know that we can disagree without our whole relationship being at stake, if I can criticize him without bringing this life-and-death intensity to the discussion, then maybe he won't be as intense in defending what he wants to do. Maybe he'll be more persuadable if he doesn't feel his independence is at stake. Maybe it will be easier for him to shake his head 'yes' to what I'm saying if he doesn't feel I'm pulling strings of guilt to make him do it."

My friends, having said what I set out to say, perhaps I had better comment on what I have not said, because I know this is an issue that touches a lot of people deeply. I have not said that parents shouldn't be concerned with their grown children's morals or their behavior. Of course they should be concerned, and they should convey their concern, make it very clear how they feel. And I have not said that children can ignore their parents' feelings. Honoring your parents is still one of the Ten Commandments. But let them do it freely, out of love, because they want to. What I've been trying to say is that communication between parents and grown children, communication between parents and their aging parents, should be honest communication between two free adults who sincerely care about each other, with no attempts on either side to control the other person through shame or guilt.

To love somebody means to respect that person's integrity as a person. Anything less than that is really loving yourself through the medium of someone else's life. In that story I told you at the beginning of this sermon, about the young boy whose mother had died when he was born, I think the father had the right to use every argument he could to persuade the boy to see things differently. But the one thing he had no right to throw into the conversation was his mother's gravestone, because how do you discuss that calmly and rationally?

Our parents don't own us and we don't own our children. As Eve found out, and as every parent has had to learn since, children don't belong to us as possessions, no matter how much we might want them to. Ultimately, everybody has to live his own life, tied to the generations before and after by bonds of loyalty and affection, but not tied by moral IOUs and strings of guilt.

Ultimately, we have to learn to give birth and to give love, to accept life and to accept love, as genuine gifts, not as loans or investments to be paid back with interest - to give for the joy of giving, with no strings attached. To be a child is to accept the responsibility of caring about your parents' feelings and their welfare, not out of guilt but out of freely given concern, out of a love that can't be bought and can't be coerced. To be a parent is to love a child because children are to be loved, because loving them fulfills you as a human being, so that one day our children will grow up to be parents themselves, and know how to love their children as parents should love children, with no strings attached.

He found a small traditional shul down the street from his lodgings. He went there for Kol Nidre services, fully intending to make it his farewell to Judaism. But when he came out three hours later, he was a changed man. Suddenly it was no longer necessary, it was no longer possible for him to change his faith.

FRANZ ROSENZWEIG COMES HOME

Kol Nidre 1970

I would like to tell you a story, a Yom Kippur story. It is the most important Yom Kippur story I know. It is the story of what happened to Franz Rosenzweig on Yom Kippur 1913. Rosenzweig was one of the important Jewish philosophers of the twentieth century, and a close friend and collaborator of Martin Buber. I confess that, although I sometimes find his philosophy hard to follow, I find his biography, his life story, utterly compelling.

Today Rosenzweig is one of the honored names in modern Jewish thought. But in the fall of 1913 he was on the verge of converting to Christianity. He grew up in a nominally Jewish home, but like so many of the intellectual Jewish families of early twentieth century Germany, there was very little that was Jewish about it. Nothing Jewish happened within the home, but annually the family would attend High Holy Day services at the local Reform Temple. Rosenzweig had nothing *against* Judaism; it just didn't seem to matter to anyone he knew.

Then he went to college. For the first time, he met deeply religious Christians, and he began to envy them. They knew who they were and what they stood for. They had a guide, they had a source of inspiration they could turn to when they were troubled. The enlightened agnostic students, Jewish and Christian alike, if they had a personal problem they could not handle, either went out and got drunk or else searched for an answer in the philosophic writings of Hegel. Either way they woke up with a headache the next morning. The religious students had a code and a way to follow.

Young Rosenzweig was impressed by the degree to which these very religious Christians were at peace with themselves. He contrasted their deeply rooted faith with the shallow pretense, the floundering inconsistency, the vulgarity and hypocrisy he had seen at home. He resolved to become a Christian. He decided that he would go to services one last time that Yom Kippur to say goodbye to his Jewish past and "graduate" to the "higher" religion.

He told his parents, and they were shocked. "What are you after?" they asked him. "How can we change Judaism so you will be willing to accept it? What can we do to make it easier, more convenient, more interesting for you?" And he told them they did not understand at all, and that he was going to do what he had to do. "Not in our shul, you don't" they said. "In our synagogue, there is no room for an apostate."

So Rosenzweig returned to Berlin, where he was studying, and found a small, traditional shul down the street from his lodgings. He went there for Kol Nidre services, fully intending to make it his farewell to Judaism. But when he came out three hours later, he was a changed man. He found something in Judaism he never knew was there before. Suddenly - as he wrote to a cousin of his afterwards - it was no longer necessary, indeed it was no longer possible for him to change his faith.

There is more to the story. Rosenzweig was drafted into the Kaiser's army in World War One. He began to work out his philosophy of religion reflecting on his experience as a soldier being shot at. He wrote a book on postcards which he mailed home from the front. He came back, began a friendship with Martin Buber, and became the mentor of young Jewish intellectuals in Germany. Then, in his thirties, he came down with a nerve disease that crippled and ultimately killed him, although he continued his creative work to his last moments.

Tonight I want to concentrate on the first part of the Rosenzweig story, the events of that Yom Kippur sixty years ago, because I think it says some things to us that we need to be told.

What happened that night in Berlin to change this man's life so completely? What happened to make him see his Jewishness in a totally new light, to plant the conviction that Judaism was not only worth holding on to, but was worth devoting his life to? I cannot believe it was merely the text of the service, which was conducted in a language he did not understand. I cannot believe that this university student, with a Ph.D. in philosophy, heard a sermon more eloquent or more intellectually stimulating than what he had heard in previous years in his parents' Temple. I cannot believe that the building was so impressive, or the choir so good, or the ushering so efficient, that it changed his life. What then, did he find there that he had never known before?

For the first time in his life, he saw a community of Jews who *cared* about their religious tradition.

He had never seen that before - not in his home, not among his relatives, not at the impressive Temple his parents took him to three times a year, and not among the other Jewish students at the university. These people in this shul were not strangers to what they were doing. They were not an audience, going to synagogue in September the way they would go to a symphony in December. They had an intensity, a sense of spiritual engagement, which he had sensed and envied when he saw it among devout Christians. He had never known that Jews were capable of this. And although he had not known it, that was what he had been missing and seeking.

What had been his objections to Judaism, objections that brought him close to renouncing it? Not that it did not make *sense*, but that it didn't *matter*. It didn't seem to transform or deepen the people who took hold of it.

I don't know if at any time during his wavering flirtation with Christianity, he ever sat down with a rabbi or some other learned

Jew who tried to explain Judaism to him. Maybe the learned authority tried to show him what a reasonable and intelligent religion Judaism was, how it agreed with the latest scientific findings, how it harmonized with Darwin, Marx, and Freud so much more easily than Christianity did.

And maybe Rosenzweig answered, "That's all very interesting, I'm sure, but I am really not impressed by the fact that Judaism makes sense. If I want something that makes sense, if I want something intellectually profound and impressive, I know where to find it. I majored in philosophy at college. That is not what I want from my religion. I am glad to hear that Judaism is not unreasonable, and that it does not offend logic. But don't you understand? That isn't enough! I want my religion to excite me, to move me. I want it to give me the courage to face darkness and illness, the strength to survive tragedy, the confidence and clarity to overcome doubt, the compassion to feel someone else's pain as if it were my own. And you sit there and tell me, 'Well maybe the sea didn't split; they walked across on a sandbar at low tide.' That is perfectly fine, but it is not worth investing my life in."

Maybe his father or mother sat down with him before that fateful Yom Kippur and tried to talk him out of it, saying to him "Couldn't you remain Jewish for our sakes, even if there isn't anything to it? We are asking so little of you. We are talking about such a small Judaism; it would be no hardship. We are not asking you to observe anything, to do anything, even to believe anything Jewish. We are just asking you to *be*."

And he might well have answered "That is exactly the problem. Why should I take seriously a religion which asks so little of me, a religion with no content, only a label, when I can find a religion which thinks enough of me, and takes me seriously enough to ask for my soul. I want to be guided, I want to have great demands made of me, and you offer me a diluted diet of 'be a nice person and come back next year.'"

Even as many bright, sensitive young people today are showing a hunger for religion, for transcendent experiences and great causes, many of them are turning away from a Judaism that asks so little of them. They are espousing those causes that perhaps do not make so much sense, but make demands, that move in and take over their lives with a quality of dedication they have been hungering for.

Franz Rosenzweig, after all, took life seriously, and he could not see the point of a religion that did not ask to be taken seriously. Yet all around him he saw Jews who said "What I like about Judaism is that you do not have to be any more Jewish than you want to be, and I do not want to be very Jewish at all."

We almost lost him to Christianity, except that one day, by accident, he stumbled into a little shul and found Jews he had never known about before, Jews for whom Judaism was more than a label; it was a great demand, it was the ruling passion of their lives. And he became one of them. He did not become orthodox; he became a very original, unconventional thinker, liberal in some ways, demanding more of himself in some ways than the orthodox did. But he became a Jew who *cared*, a Jew who traced himself back to Mount Sinai, and who allowed that fact to shape much of his life.

Rosenzweig's experience in that Berlin synagogue teaches us something very important: Judaism is not primarily an idea; it is primarily a religious community. It is not one person at a time contemplating God; it is people interacting, treating each other humanly, sharing and striving for something together. Judaism is the Jewish *people* as much as it is Jewish belief. And what ultimately "converted" Rosenzweig back to Judaism (if I can use that term) was the impact of Jewish community - real live people turned on by the reality of their Jewishness.

Remember, Rosenzweig was a philosopher by profession. He took ideas seriously; he probed and argued ideas. But ultimately he had to discover that a person's life is not shaped only by ideas; it is shaped by the other people he meets. Ideas, however profound or important they may be, are abstract until a person makes them real by living them. Even God is only an idea until people make Him real in this world by doing godly things, by basing their actions on what He stands for.

An example: Rosenzweig as a young man had read about the idea of the Sabbath, and was never terribly impressed by it. But he had never seen one. He had never seen anybody really experiencing Shabbat. After his return to Judaism, he saw Shabbat live, the idea translated into action, and he was overwhelmed.

That is the story. Why have I told it to you? For several reasons. I wanted you to know that it is possible for a person's whole life to change in one day - or, if not his whole life, at least the direction of his life, so that as he keeps on growing and developing, he is growing in a new direction. That is what *Teshuvah*, repentance, really means; not merely regretting or apologizing or groveling. It means "turning," giving yourself a new direction, a new orientation. Rosenzweig, in his later years, used to speak of "the ladder of observance." How do you make yourself more of a Jew? How do you bring Judaism significantly into your life? The same way you climb a ladder, not in great big jumps, but one step up at a time, higher and higher.

I have told you this story too because I am continually telling *myself* the story. Whenever I get up to conduct a service, I say to myself "What if there is a Franz Rosenzweig here today? What if there is a bright, thoughtful young person who wants to give Judaism one more chance before he gives up on it, one more chance to show that it is not as vapid, as mindless or as superficial as he has always seen it to be? How is he going to react? What is he going to go away with?"

I realize it is not enough for *me* to know the story; *you* have to know it too. Because it is not up to me alone. Franz Rosenzweig was not saved by a good sermon, a series of original modern prayers, or a persuasive intellectual argument. He was saved for Judaism by the life-giving encounter with a congregation of Jews who brought Judaism to life and made it real and powerful. And that is where you come in, except that you probably feel miscast. You would feel more comfortable playing the role of Rosenzweig than playing the observant congregation. That is exactly the problem. We are all Rosenzweig, we and our children. We have read about Judaism, we have heard about Judaism, we may know a few intensely Jewish individuals. But we have never seen a real live Jewish community.

We know what it is like to come to services and be part of the audience, to admire the Bar Mitzvah boy, to follow the page announcements and the English readings, and to wait patiently and politely for the end. But do any of us know what it is like to be part of a congregation and not just an audience, a congregation that is really praying, responding, celebrating, so that you forget that you are an isolated individual and become one limb of a great organism in the presence of God? No wonder we have such a distorted idea of the value of congregational worship!

Some of us may have grown up in homes that were filled with a sense of Jewishness twenty-four hours a day - Yiddish, *davvening*, kosher meals, paying attention to news articles about Eretz Yisrael or to Jewish names in the press. Something Jewish was happening all the time. Will any of our children have that experience? At best, there will be isolated moments of Jewishness, once or twice a week, maybe only once or twice a year, like the home in which Franz Rosenzweig was raised.

Can we blame our children for thinking of Judaism as an occasional garment to be dusted off and worn for special occasions? You know how today's young people are about getting dressed up for special occasions!

We send them to religious school to learn about Judaism, and when that does not turn them into Jews, we blame the teacher, we blame the Temple, we blame ourselves and our children. But we never realize where the fault really lies.

Books alone do not make good Jews out of children. Assemblies, songs, projects cannot do it by themselves. What shapes people into Jews? The thing that shaped Franz Rosenzweig: a vibrant Jewish community for them to emulate and grow into, and become a part of. And there simply is no such Jewish community around here today. There are a lot of Jews coming together, but there is no sense of community.

My friends, it is the eve of Yom Kippur again. It is the time to re-enact the drama of Franz Rosenzweig, the most important, most relevant Yom Kippur story I know. The only trouble is that there are so many of us qualified to play the part of Rosenzweig, and so few of us prepared to play the committed Jewish community that wins him back. How do you change that ratio?

How can we create a Jewish community out of a lot of well-meaning, well-intentioned but unconnected individual Jews? I think one key is Rosenzweig's ladder of observance. You get yourself a new direction, a new orientation, and then you progress one step at a time. And since we are all starting from about the same point, if we all move in the same direction, we *become* a community. We are no longer Rosenzweigs, lonely individuals in search. We are the Jewish people on the move, doing Jewish things *together.*

I do not think the Temple can convert people, because a Temple is only a building. You need a congregation to convert people, and I am not sure we have that yet. But the Temple building can offer a meeting place, a place for people in search to come together, to try to find each other. And that too may be a start.

If we could have a nucleus of people saying "Skin-deep Judaism never did anything for me; I would like to find out if soul-deep Judaism is any different," if they could do that as a group, strengthening and reinforcing each other, and minimizing the self-consciousness that is always a part of doing something new, we might just do it. We might see history repeat itself.

The Hasidim tell the story of how, when the Jews were in danger, the Baal Shem Tov would go to a certain spot in the forest. There he would light a fire, and sing a certain melody; and his prayers would be answered.

In later years, his disciple who had seen him do this no longer knew the melody. But he would go to the same place, light the fire, and *his* prayers would be answered. *His* disciple, in time of danger, would go to the same place in the forest, although he did not know the melody and could not light the fire. And because God is merciful, He would answer his prayers too. *His* disciple, the fourth generation, would pray in his heart, "Lord of the Universe, I no longer know the melody, I cannot light the fire, and I cannot find the place in the forest. All I can do is tell the story. Please let that be enough."

I think that is our predicament. We do not have the kind of magic that saved Franz Rosenzweig for Judaism. We do not know the song and we do not have the fire. So we do the only thing we can. We tell the story, and we pray that it will be enough, and that the same miracle that saved Franz Rosenzweig for Judaism, *Bayamim hahem bazman hazeh,* at this season of Kol Nidre many years ago, happen once again to us.

REMEMBER US.

Remember us because the only place

we still live in this world is in your

memories. We don't live at the cemetery.

You can't find us in a photo album or on

a memorial plaque. The only place we

live in this world is in your heart.

GHOSTS

Yom Kippur 2005

It will probably never happen again in my lifetime. It may never happen again in your lifetime. So I think it is worth taking sermonic notice of the fact that this year Yom Kippur falls only nineteen days before Halloween. It's more than just a quirk of the calendar. What is the connection between Yom Kippur and Halloween? Yom Kippur is the one day of the year when the synagogue is haunted. Tonight and tomorrow we will sense the presence in shul of the spirits of the departed, people who were once part of our lives and are no longer physically among us. We will feel their presence not only during Yizkor. We will find ourselves thinking of them when we come in to find our seats and remember times when they sat next to us. They will be on our minds when we recite the prayer "who shall live and who shall die, who in the fullness of their years and who before their time," and we will remember other years, other Yom Kippur services when that prayer forced us to contemplate the fact that our parents were getting older and we wondered how many more Yom Kippurs we would have with them. We will remember other years, other High Holy Day services when maybe we had a sick husband or wife at home, or maybe a brother or sister or even a child was in the hospital and the Mahzor's prayers about life and death merged with our prayers for their recovery.

There will be ghosts walking the aisles of the synagogue during the service tonight and tomorrow. Listen to what they have come to say to us. Don't be afraid to listen to them, for fear that they have come to nag or criticize us the way they may have done when they were alive. The world they now inhabit is a world without complaints, without anger. It is a world that knows only truth and love. So listen to them.

The first thing they have come to say to us is, "Remember us. Remember us because the only place we still live in this world is in your memories. We don't live at the cemetery. You can't find us in a photo album or on a memorial plaque. The only place we live in this world is in your heart. Illness, death took us out of your world physically but you have the power to keep us present, to keep the essential part of us alive emotionally by remembering us. Pass on our names, tell your children and grandchildren about us and you will help us to overcome death and find our way back in the only way we can to the land of the living."

They are saying to us, "Remember us for your own sakes as well as for ours. You forfeit such a large part of your identity if you erase us from your sense of who you are. Like the person suffering from Alzheimer's Disease who can't lead a meaningful life because he has lost that sense of who he is, you will never really understand who you are if you leave us out of the equation. Remembering us is not something you do for us; it's a favor you do yourself. You can't understand who you are, where you come from, why you do some of the things you do if you try to forget the people who were once a large part of your life.

"Remember us, because when you do so, you act as a role model for those around you. You teach your children and everyone who knows you how to hold on to people you love and lose. Remembering us is your insurance policy for your own immortality, the knowledge that people will remember you and attach your name to a blessing even as you do for us."

The ghosts that populate the synagogue tonight and tomorrow are saying to us, "Remember us in love. Even if some of the memories we left behind are hard ones, even if some of them are painful, let the good memories prevail. If there is bitterness, if there were disappointments, if you find yourself wishing you had had different parents, wishing your marriage had turned out differently, wishing you had gotten along better with some of your family, please cleanse your soul of all that bitterness. It's too late to do anything about the past, so why let it infect your soul with unhappiness and regret?"

They are saying, "If we made mistakes years ago, it was because we were amateurs in an area where even the experts don't always know what is right. But remember, the word "amateur" doesn't only mean "unqualified." "Amateur" comes from the same root as the word "amorous." It means doing things for love. Even our mistakes were done out of love."

There was a book that came out a year or two ago by George Vaillant, titled *Aging Well*. It's the third and final volume of a long-term study initiated at Harvard that tried to identify those traits of personality in young people that seemed to forecast a happy and successful life. Dr. Vaillant identifies two things that correlate with a satisfying last third of a person's life, and I think they are important enough to apply even to people for whom a satisfying old age is a far-off prospect that you shouldn't have to worry about for decades.

One was the ability to make new friends as old friends die or move away. That way, your social network keeps growing instead of shrinking. You feel your world getting larger instead of smaller. Especially if you find yourself in an empty nest or moving from a house to an apartment, you need to know that your social world is expanding even as your physical world may be contracting. Vaillant suggests that you check in on yourself every six to twelve months, asking "Have I made a new friend recently or am I limiting myself to the same shrinking group of people I've known for years?"

The second and more important trait is the willingness to forgive people you're upset with and angry at, some of them still living and others long gone. He defines forgiveness as the recognition that it's too late to have a better past, and points out that holding on to grudges rarely hurts the person we're angry at but eats away at us. It's like the woman who came to see me some years ago, after I had given a Yom Kippur sermon on the theme of forgiveness. She told me how her husband had left her for a younger woman some years before, and how ever since then she has had to work two jobs to pay the bills. She described having to tell her children there was no money to go to the movies or buy video games, and then she said to me, "And you want me to forgive him for what he did to us?"

I told her, "That's right. I want you to forgive him, – not because he deserves it, not because what he did was all right. I understand that sometimes the only power you have over someone who has mistreated you is the power to withhold forgiveness, to keep your anger on life support and not let it die a natural death. But look at what you're doing to yourself. You're not hurting him. He's living it up with his new family in another state, and your simmering anger just convinces him that he had good reason to leave. For ten years, you've been standing here in Natick holding a hot coal in your hand, waiting for your ex to come by so you could throw it at him, and all you've done is burn your hand. It's in your own best interest to put the coal down and go on with your life."

Some of you may know that I've been working on a book about the life of Moses. The last chapter is devoted to the last great achievement of Moses' life: that he wasn't angry at God for the way his life turned out. He could have been. The Israelites who had made his life difficult with their demands and their complaints were about to enter the Promised Land, and Moses would never get to do that. The burden of leadership had taken its toll on his family. He could have been angry at God but he chose not to. He could have resented other people for getting to do what he would never get to do, but he chose not to do that either. The Torah ends, in its last two chapters, with Moses' hymn of praise to God and his blessing of the twelve tribes of Israel.

I have known too many people in and out of this congregation who could not enjoy the last third of their lives because they were angry at God for the way their lives had turned out, for all the things they yearned for that they never got, the recognition, the promotions, the family nachas. And I felt sorry for them. They perversely kept on hoping for a better past. It never occurred to them that, over and above what life had denied them, they were denying themselves that final blessing of living their days out in peace and contentment.

Some of the ghosts that will be haunting the congregation tonight and tomorrow aren't sure how welcome they will be when they come to us, when they try to infiltrate our minds. They are hoping that we will recognize that what is past is past, that we will let go of old grudges and resentments, – why be angry, why be jealous of someone who is no longer alive? – and that we will welcome them wholeheartedly.

The ghosts who come here tonight are saying, "Remember us. Remember us even if some of the memories are painful, memories of illness and of helplessness in the face of illness, memories of words unspoken that should have been spoken and words spoken that would have been better withheld, because you can't hold on to the good memories, the golden hours, without the sad memories tagging along as well."

Have you noticed that in the last few years, there have been a number of movies about people losing their memories? Some of them are comedies, like the Adam Sandler movie in which his girl friend meets him every day unable to remember that she has ever seen him before. Some are dramas; a person has had something terrible done to him but he can't remember why or by whom, and he has to find out. Some are science fiction; a man who knows too much has his memory erased. I find myself wondering why this theme all of a sudden, and

I can think of two reasons over and above the obvious one that, in Hollywood, when one movie does well, it inspires a dozen copies.

For one thing, in this age of computers, we can delete obsolete computer files to make room for new data. One scientist I know explains the fact that around age fourteen, we lose our ability to learn new languages by comparing the human mind to a computer that erases certain skills to free up capacity for new challenges. But I think there may be another reason, a more important one. So many people are walking around burdened by painful memories, victims of war and discrimination, victims of crime and betrayal, people hurt by someone close to them, people ashamed of something they have done, and they wish they could wash their minds clean of those painful memories.

In my opinion, the most interesting of the memory–loss movies was called "Eternal Sunshine of the Spotless Mind." It's the story of a young man and a young woman who meet, are attracted to each other and have a brief, passionate affair before they break up. They find their breakup so unbearably painful that first the girl, then the young man agree to undergo a radical procedure to erase their memories of each other. The premise of the movie is that a psychiatrist has found a way of locating precisely where in the brain a specific memory is stored and destroying that memory. At one point, as he is undergoing the treatment to erase his memories of the girl, the young man summons up a memory of a time they were together and he is saying to her, "This is the happiest I have ever been in my life." The thought suddenly occurs to him, "Why do I want to erase the memory of the happiest I have ever been?" and he begins to fight the treatment.

That is the challenge the ghosts of Yom Kippur set before us: the painful memories of love and loss are inextricably tied to some of the most precious memories we own, and we can't hold on to one without letting the other into our minds as well. It's like the passage in the prayer by Rabbi Morris Adler that we sometimes read at the Yizkor service:

> "Shall I grieve for a youth that has gone once my
> hair is gray and my shoulders bent,
> And forget the days of vibrancy and power...?
> Shall the time of darkness put out forever the glow
> of the light in which I once walked?"

Naomi Shemer, the beloved Israeli composer who died last year, is best known for writing *Yerushalayim shel Zahav*, Jerusalem of Gold, shortly before the Six-Day War in 1967. A few years later, she wrote another very popular song called *Al HaD'vash v'al Ha-Oketz*, For the Honey and the Sting. The title comes from a story in the Talmud about a man who sticks his hand into a beehive to take the honeycomb and is stung by the bees. He walks away muttering, "I can do without the honey and without the sting." Naomi Shemer says just the opposite. She says, "No, I want the honey. I want to taste the goodness, the sweetness of life. I want to know the joy of love, of family, of trying to do things that matter. And if the only way I can have those things is to leave myself vulnerable to the bees, I welcome the honey and the stings."

In the same vein, the ghosts that come to visit us on Yom Kippur are saying to us, "We bring you memories of honey and of bee stings, memories of days that warm your heart and days that break your heart. And we come to remind you that you can't have one without the other."

Finally, the ghosts that haunt the synagogue on Yom Kippur have one more message for us, perhaps the most important thing they would say to us today: Don't envy us. Don't be in a hurry to join us, just because we inhabit a world where there is no pain, no disease, no conflict, no betrayal. Don't ever be in a hurry to join us. No matter how painful, no matter how frustrating or unsatisfying your life may be, cherish every day of it, because once you let go of it, there is no getting it back. You've never been dead, they are saying to us, but we've been alive, and believe us, alive is better.

I remember a cartoon I saw some years ago. It shows a husband and wife who have died and gone to heaven. And heaven is bright sunshine and soft music and it's so peaceful. The husband turns to his wife and says, "Just think, if we hadn't given up smoking and eaten all that oat bran, we could have had all this ten years sooner."

The ghosts of Yom Kippur come to tell us, "Don't believe that. Given our choice, we'd rather be alive in a world of love and a world of pain, in a world of achievement and a world of disappointment and frustration, in a world of honey and a world of wounds. Alive is better."

Last spring, when the tragic case of Terri Schiavo was dominating the news, someone asked me what I thought about it, and I answered that I thought everyone was wrong. The parents were wrong for persisting in their denial as to how sick their daughter was, refusing to listen to doctors because they didn't like what the doctors were telling them. The voices of the religious right were wrong for saying, in effect, "we own the government, we own the Congress and the courts, and when we tell them to jump, they better jump or else." The politicians were nothing short of despicable for jumping on command and then, when the poll numbers came in, jumping the other way.

But I thought the most wrong of all were the people who said, "Anytime life becomes too painful for a person, he or she should have the right to end it." I'm not talking about someone in an irreversible coma, in a persistent vegetative state, a person who has essentially finished living and is in the process of dying. My own living will states that, should I no longer be aware of what is happening to me or around me, should I no longer be aware of the people around me, with no chance of recovery, I don't want the dying process to be prolonged.

But carried to extremes, the right to die leads to incidents like that of the writer Hunter Thompson or of his role model Ernest Hemingway, taking their own lives for no reason except that life wasn't fun any more. Who ever guaranteed that life would always be fun? That sense of giving up so readily underestimates the strength of ordinary people, their ability to live with pain and to keep going despite the pain. Whom do we admire more, Hunter Thompson who despairs of life and leaves his family to pick up the pieces of what he did, or Christopher Reeve who was in a much worse situation and found the strength to go on because he was surrounded by people who gave him a reason to get up every morning. And the good news is that you don't have to be Superman to do what Christopher Reeve did. Many of us have seen instances of that in our own families and they have inspired us to resist the message that when life gets hard, give up.

The voices from the other world come to tell us, "A life of pain is still a life full of things too precious to give up on. Turn to the people around you to ease the pain, to remind you of why you want to live through the night and wake up again tomorrow morning, because your world contains people who are important to you," because this world is under the sovereignty of a God who is *melech hafetz b'hayyim*, a God who treasures life and who wants us to treasure life. They would urge us to see every day, no matter what kind of day, no matter the weather, no matter the prognosis, as a gift. "What we would give," they are saying to us, "for one more day of food and sunshine, of hugs and embraces." The rabbis of the Talmud tell us that one hour in this world is worth more than eternity in the World to Come.

My friends, there will be moments during the Yom Kippur service when the voices you hear will not be my voice or the cantor's voice or the voices of several hundred people chanting around you. They will be voices from your past, voices from beyond, not urging you to join them but pleading to join you, asking to be remembered, speaking of love and memory and forgiveness, of pain and courage. Listen to those voices and may they be the voices, more than mine, more than the cantor's, to which we will answer. AMEN.

"I AM GOING TO SEND YOU the prophet Elijah

just before the dawning of the messianic

age, and he will help bring about the one

thing the world is lacking to make it the

messianic kingdom. He will connect the

hearts of parents to their children, and

the hearts of children to their parents.

He will teach us to love again, and

then the world will be redeemed."

JACOB'S FEARS AND OURS

Yom Kippur 2006

A man came up to me one evening after one of my lectures and said to me, "Rabbi, you seem to know the Bible pretty well. Can you tell me, of all the things that God says to people in the Bible, what sentence does God repeat more often than any other?" I thought for a moment and said, "Probably the one about being kind to the widow, the stranger and the poor person. I think God says that eight or nine times in the Torah." He shook his head and said, "Not even close. The sentence God repeats more than any other is: Don't be afraid."

I checked it out when I got home and it turns out he was right. More than eighty times, God says *al tira*, "fear not," don't be afraid. He says it to Abraham, to Isaac, to Jacob. He says it to every one of the prophets and tells them to say it to the people. I believe God is trying to get that message to us today: Don't be afraid when you read the news coming out of the Middle East. Don't be afraid when you hear about the problems facing American society. It's not that there is nothing to be afraid of. There are lots of things to be afraid of, but God wants to reassure us that we can handle them if we are not paralyzed by fear.

For forty days before Yom Kippur and for ten days afterward, we add a psalm to our daily prayers every morning and evening, a psalm we don't recite at any other time of the year. It begins *Adonai Ori V'yish'i, mi-mi ira, Adonai ma'oz hayyai, mi-mi efchad*? God is my light and my salvation; whom shall I fear? God is the source of my strength; of what shall I be afraid?

Now, when the psalmist tells us three times in the first three lines that he's not afraid, the message we hear is that he *is* afraid but he is working at coping with his fears, and that he turns to God to help him do that, just as the author of the 23rd Psalm writes, "I shall fear no evil *for Thou art with me.*"

Eighty times God tells our ancestors not to be afraid. I want to focus on one of those times this evening. When I verified the claim about that being the sentence occurring most frequently in the Bible, I shared that insight with my friend Rabbi Jack Riemer, and he responded by sharing with me an insight into one occurrence of that phrase.

It happened to Jacob late in his life. You may remember the story from the Bible. Jacob had twelve sons. He favored one of them, Joseph, over the others, and in their jealousy, the other brothers sold him as a slave to a passing caravan and told their father that he had been killed by a wild animal. Joseph ended up in Egypt where he interpreted Pharaoh's dreams, advised him on how to avoid a famine and made Egypt the only country in the area with enough food for its people and a surplus to sell to foreigners. Joseph's brothers came to buy food, and Joseph revealed his identity to them twenty years after they had sold him into slavery. He invited them and their by-now-elderly father to move to Egypt where he would provide for them.

The brothers then return home and tell Jacob that Joseph is alive, that he is an important government official in Egypt and that he wants them to move there to live with him. Jacob immediately begins to make plans to relocate his family to Egypt.

It is at this point that God appears to Jacob. God hasn't spoken to him once in the past twenty years, which the midrash explains by saying that the spirit of God does not abide with a person when he is grieving or angry. God says to Jacob, *al tira*, don't be afraid. God makes three promises to Jacob: I will go down to Egypt with you, I will bring you and your family back, and your son Joseph will close your eyes.

I want to focus on those three promises, because God understands even before Jacob does what Jacob is afraid of.

First, "Don't be afraid to go down to Egypt because I will be with you." Jacob is about to enter a new stage in his life. He doesn't know what is in store for him, but he does know two things: change is inevitable and change is scary. Change means leaving the familiar for the unknown. Once before, you may remember, God spoke to Jacob when he was leaving the familiar for the unknown. It happened when he was an adolescent leaving home because he had cheated his brother Esau and deceived his father to gain the blessing that was meant for his brother. That time, God reassured him that, although he was leaving his parents' home and leaving the land of Canaan, he was not leaving God behind. God would be accessible to him at the house of Laban as God had been at his parents' home.

Now once again, many years and many experiences later, Jacob is about to leave the land of Canaan and make his way to a new land. This time he is not exchanging adolescence for adult responsibility, as he did the first time he left home, facing the uncertainties of marriage, parenthood, earning a living and establishing his identity. This time, he is exchanging the role of head of the household, being a mature adult responsible for his own well-being and that of those around him, for the role of an old man in an unfamiliar setting, sustained and supported by others. That scares him, and that is why God comes to him now and reassures him, "Don't be afraid."

Now do you see why I chose this passage to focus on? It's Yom Kippur, when we recite the prayer about "what is the New Year going to be like? A year of health and prosperity, or a year of illness and financial concern? A year of new people coming into our lives, or a year of people leaving us?" There are people here this evening who are facing the same kind of uncertainty that Jacob faced in the Bible. Maybe they are contemplating changing jobs, even changing careers. Maybe their children are grown and they are thinking of selling their home and moving into smaller quarters, and at some level it gives them the feeling that their world is shrinking. There are people here this evening who look at the horizon and see the end of their working life approaching, or perhaps they are wondering how much longer their current job will be viable. And they are asking themselves, as Jacob must have been asking himself, Who will I be when I am no longer bringing home a paycheck? Who will I be when I'm no longer in charge of a household and a family? There are people here this evening for whom the coming year will represent a new family arrangement, some of you adding, some of you subtracting, and you are understandably apprehensive about how that will work out.

God doesn't answer Jacob's concerns directly, but He does answer them when He says "I will go down to Egypt with you." God is saying, "Yes, the future is unknown. The future is by definition always unknown. But you have to believe that, whatever the future holds, you will be up to the challenge. Look at what you've already done. You've worked your way through problems before. I was with you in hard times in Aram and in Canaan, and I'm not about to abandon you now."

God says to Jacob, "Don't think only about what you are leaving behind. Think of the new experiences awaiting you, and the opportunities for growth and for remaining vital that these new experiences will represent, because facing and mastering new situations will keep you young and vital."

God's second promise, "I will bring you and your offspring back," speaks to Jacob's second fear. If Jacob was afraid, on the one hand, that Egypt would not work out as a home for him and his family, that they would not fit in, at the same time, he is afraid that it might work out all too well, that his children and grandchildren will feel too much at home in Egypt and forget that they are the descendants of Abraham, Isaac and Jacob. And again you see why this is a passage that speaks to us today. We have been accepted in America, integrated into American life, more than our parents and grandparents could ever have imagined. My father spent the first twenty years of his life in Lithuania, but he never thought of himself as Lithuanian. He didn't speak Lithuanian, he spoke Hebrew and Yiddish. Even more so, the Jews of Germany, who did speak German, wrote important books in German, contributed to the cultural life of Germany, in fact virtually *were* the cultural life of Germany, were never permitted to forget that they were part of a separate community. But in this country in the past fifty years, we have been accepted. The bigots, the anti-Semites have been marginalized. If two generations ago, Jack Benny and Danny Kaye had to change their names to make it in show business, nobody asked that of Jerry Seinfeld or Barbra Streisand. We have been accepted and we are grateful for it. But at the same time, we share Jacob's fear. We worry that our children and grandchildren will become so assimilated – in the clothes they wear, in the music they listen to, in the pop stars they idolize—that they will forget that they are Jewish. God's promise is that they may wander, they may find an Egypt to travel to psychologically, but they will find their way back. If God's Covenant with Abraham is true, if the Revelation at Sinai is true, the truth will ultimately win out. People will come to recognize it. If the bond between parents and children is strong, if we don't overreact to an adolescent slamming the door to her room by slamming doors of our own, then that bond will exert a gravitational pull strong enough to keep them from wandering too far.

And it seems to me to be happening. Thirty years ago, bright young Jews were traveling to India and Nepal to study Buddhism. Today, non-Jewish Hollywood celebrities are studying Kabbalah. There are serious books being written, college courses being offered, adult classes proliferating, creative options for worship and study, to a degree that we have never seen before. Who could have foreseen a generation ago that Chabad houses would be as ubiquitous as Starbucks? In the spiritual world as in the culinary world, people are coming to realize that junk food may be tempting but is ultimately harmful, and are finding their way back to the real thing.

There is a Jewish legend about how Sh'ma Yisrael became the quintessential declaration of Jewish faith. It bases itself on an incident at the very end of the book of Genesis, the very end of Jacob's life in Egypt. Jacob is dying. He calls Joseph to his bedside and asks Joseph to bring his children, Jacob's grandchildren, so that he can bless them. Jacob then goes on at great length praising his grandchildren, telling Joseph how much he loves them, as if they were his own children. Then, the Bible says, he looks at Joseph's children, Menasseh and Ephraim, and asks, "*Mi eleh*? Who are those kids?" And Joseph has to explain to him, "Those are the children with whom God has blessed me."

According to the Midrash, why doesn't Jacob recognize his own grandchildren, the ones he has just been talking about, saying how much he loves them? Not because his eyesight is failing, as happened to his father Isaac. He doesn't recognize them because they look like Egyptian children. Born and raised in Egypt, their dress, their appearance is no different from the young people around them. And that bothers Jacob deeply. When he asks, "Who are those young people?", he is really asking "I know what their names are, but who are they? Are they Jewish children? Are they part of our family, part of our people, with the same commitments and loyalties? Or have they become Egyptian children with Jewish parents?"

And Menasseh and Ephraim, sensing their grandfather's concern, answer him, *Sh'ma Yisrael*, Listen, Grandpa Israel (remember, Jacob's other name is Israel), *Adonai Eloheynu,* the Lord is our God. We may look different, we may act different, but we still believe in the same God, the same Covenant, the same values, the same bloodstained and tear-stained history that you do. And ever since then, Jewish parents have blessed their sons on the eve of the Sabbath, saying "May you be like Ephraim and Menasseh, fully integrated into the society you live in and at the same time, loyal and learned members of the Jewish people." As God is immortal, as the Torah is immortal, God's promise that the Jewish people will continue to be His representative on earth, that He will guide them to find their way back from whatever Egypt they have wandered to, is equally eternal.

God's third promise to Jacob is perhaps the most interesting and the most relevant of the three. "Joseph will close your eyes." Do you understand the reference? When a person dies, if he should die with his eyes open, the final act of kindness one can perform for him is to close his eyes, to bring down the final curtain on his life.

What is Jacob worried about as he prepares to relocate to Egypt? He hasn't spoken to Joseph for twenty years, since the day he disappeared and was presumed dead. I imagine Jacob thinking to himself, "How does he feel about me after all these years? Is he angry with me for neglecting him? Does he blame me for favoring him and making his brothers jealous? Has he made a new life for himself that has no room for me in it?"

I can imagine Jacob saying to himself, "There were so many times when I wasn't a very good father, when I made mistakes, when I had my priorities wrong. Will Joseph take this opportunity to get even with me?" And the greatest fear, the one he can't even put into words, is: I don't want to die alone, with nobody caring for me."

Over the years, you have told me your stories: stories of estrangements, of family members not speaking to each other, of feuds going back so many years that nobody remembers how they started. There were the funerals where families would sit shiva in two or three different homes because the brothers and sisters didn't get along and they weren't going to let their Momma's death change that. There was the woman who told me that she wasn't going to say kaddish for the father who had abused her physically and psychologically, and I tried to persuade her to say Kaddish, not to mourn the man who died but to grieve for the father she always wanted to have and never did, and now it was too late. There was even one funeral I officiated where the surviving children couldn't agree on how the family name was pronounced. Sometimes the encounter with mortality forces people to open their eyes and realize what they are missing; sometimes it finds the fault line in a family and drives people further apart.

You came to me with your stories: the elderly parent who accepted the invitation to move in with her children, only to find herself left alone all day with the dog and the television set in a town with no public transportation; the elderly parent who lived with her children and grandchildren but couldn't get her daughter to accommodate her food limitations; and at the other end, the couples who invited a widowed parent to live with them with the best will in the world, only to find themselves with no privacy and an endlessly needy parent. And behind all the stories lies the desperate, unspoken fear: I don't want to die alone. Elderly parents are understandably frightened as they grow old and dependent: will this be payback time for every argument, every restriction, every resentment held onto for decades or long buried but revived at this moment?

So Jacob is frightened as he prepares to move to Egypt to live with Joseph, and God has to reassure him. God has to say to him, Your father Isaac wasn't a very good father. He favored your brother Esau over you. He never appreciated the things that made you special, the qualities that made you the rightful heir to the tradition of Abraham. He didn't know how to help you get what you wanted and needed in life. And you weren't a very good son. You lied to him, you deceived him. You sided with your mother against him. But in the end, you came back and were able to love him. You and Esau outgrew your conflicts and when he died, the two of you came together to bury him and mourn for him. Reconciliation is possible.

Forgiveness is possible. It may not be easy but it can happen, and it is so much better than the alternative.

And then finally that moment comes. Jacob makes the long journey to Egypt. Joseph is there to welcome him. What were they thinking at that moment? Was Joseph thinking, "I can't remember what it was like to have a father, a loving father who cared for who I was and not just what I could do for him?" Was Jacob thinking, "How will Joseph handle this role reversal, my being dependent on him?"

Jacob arrives in Egypt and Joseph is there to greet him. They embrace, they kiss, they cry. And Jacob responds to Joseph's embrace by saying *amuta hapa'am*, Now I can die, which I take to mean: Now I'm not afraid of facing the end of my life, because I know I won't be facing it alone. The love that had lain dormant below the surface for all those years is recovered in one moment of mutual need and mutual forgiveness. Jacob settles into life in Egypt. Joseph presents him in court. He is proud of his father. And when Jacob dies, Joseph is there to close his eyes and tend to his burial.

My friends, it's Yom Kippur. It is the day when we spend the whole day in shul trying to plaster over the cracks in our lives, trying to put together the pieces of our lives so that we will start the New Year whole and not broken. And of all the things that frighten us, of all the dire things the New Year may have in store for us, from terrorism in this country to war in the Middle East, from loss of health to loss of jobs, I suspect that there is no prospect more frightening than the fear that we won't be able to tear down the walls that have somehow sprung up between us and other people in our lives and that, when problems come along, we'll have to face them alone.

But if the challenge is tearing down the walls that separate us, if the challenge is building bridges to re-connect us to people we really care about, that is one challenge we will not have to face alone. God promises us, as He promised Jacob, that He wants us to do it, that He understands how intimidating a prospect it is, to make ourselves vulnerable to rejection as the inevitable risk of letting yourself care for someone, but He will be with us to give us the courage.

The last words ever spoken by a prophet in Israel, the last line of the last chapter of the last of the biblical prophets Malachi, reads: *Hiney Anochi sholeach lachem et Eliya Ha-Navi*, I am going to send you the prophet Elijah just before the dawning of the messianic era, *V'heshiv lev avot el banim v'lev banim el avotam*, and he will help bring about the one thing the world is lacking to make it the messianic kingdom. He will connect the hearts of parents to their children and the hearts of children to their parents. He will teach us to love each other again, and then the world will be ready to be redeemed.

God's promise to us at the outset of a New Year is the same promise He extended to Jacob many years ago, not that it will be a year free of problems, free of conflict. It will be a year with its share of problems, change and conflict and uncertainty – but we will be up to the challenge because whenever we set out to do the right thing, God will be at our side until all that is broken will be made whole again.

FAMILY

This was one of the first sermons
I gave after assuming the pulpit in Natick,
at the age of thirty-one. It sounds themes
that would re-occur in my preaching
over the next decades.

WE HAVE THE RIGHT TO ASK, "Where was God in 1940?" but we have the duty to ask, "Where was Man? What could he have done to prevent the Holocaust?"

THE FIRST QUESTION

Yom Kippur 1966

What was the first question ever asked in the world? We cannot really know that for sure, of course. It is lost in the mist of unrecorded beginnings. But in the Bible's poetic reconstruction of how the world began, the first question came after Adam and Eve had disobeyed God's will by eating the fruit of the forbidden tree.

"Adam and his wife heard the sound of God in the garden and they hid themselves from God's presence among the trees of the garden. And the Lord God called out to Adam and said, "Where are you?"

That is the first question, God asking Man "where are you?" The midrash raises a question that may have occurred to you: Why does God have to ask where Man is? If He is God, wouldn't He know the answer? It answers its own question: of course God knows where Man was hiding, but as a good teacher might do, He asked anyway, to find out if Man knew where he was, if Man realized that in the midst of the big, beautiful world that had been given him, he was cowering behind a tree.

Yom Kippur is a day for going back and asking that first question all over again, "Where is Man?" After all the years that he has lived, where is he? What has he accomplished? Has he learned to enjoy the world, or does the thought of God still make him cower in shame? Where is Man at the end of a year of running and striving and knocking himself out? Where is he in relation to where he was last year at this time?

One contemporary rabbi puts it this way: The mood of Yom Kippur is not algebra, — What is Man? How much does he add up to?

Rather, it is calculus, Where is Man? How is he changing, and what is he in the process of becoming?

When we are confronted with evil and tragedy, we instinctively ask, "Where is God? How could He let such a thing happen?" Today we are reminded that the first question is still, "Where is Man? Why does *he* let such things happen? What has he done, of all that he might have done, to keep such things from happening?"

Sigmund Freud's biographer tells the story of how a prominent Viennese surgeon meeting Freud in the hospital where they both served, showed Freud a bone eaten away by cancer, taken from a patient whose life he had been unable to save. The surgeon said with great vehemence, "If I ever come face to face with God, I'll stick this in His face and ask Him why He created something like this in His world." And Freud answered him, "If I ever have that opportunity, I'll ask God not why He permits cancer but why He didn't give me or you or someone the intelligence to find a cure for it."

Before we permit ourselves to complain "Where is God?" let us ask the first question, "Where is Man?" What is he doing with the world God gave him? Is he spending one-tenth as much money on medical research to cure cancer or birth defects as he spends on liquor and cigarettes? Can a bright young medical researcher look forward to being paid as well as a mediocre athlete or movie star? What are we spending on behalf of the aged or the infirm, compared to what we spend to keep ourselves looking young and fit? Do we revere and respect the sacred trust of good health that we were given, or do we neglect and abuse our health and then ask, "How could God let this happen to me?" Before we turn to God with complaints about how much sickness there is in the world, let us answer first questions first.

I believe the most important challenge to theology in our lifetime is World War Two and the Holocaust. I think every religion has to go back and amend its teachings in the light of what Auschwitz has to tell us about God and Man. I know that there are a lot of people, including some of our finest, most sensitive people, who find themselves asking, "Where was God, that such things could happen?" It is a legitimate question, a very important question. But it seems to me that there is an equally valid question that ought to be asked first: Where was Man?

When Hitler was publicly proclaiming his vicious racist policies, why did people agree to accept him as a leader? Where was Man when the voters of Germany said, "Better Hitler with his peculiar ideas about Jews, than inflation or socialism?" Where was Man when Hitler came to power and actually began to carry out his insane threats? One German preacher was quoted as saying, "When they went after Jews, I did not protest because I was not a Jew. When they went after gypsies and communists, I did not protest because I was not a gypsy or a communist. When they went after labor unions, I did not protest because I was not a union member. And then when they came for me, there was no one to protest because it was too late."

Where were the lawyers, the judges, the doctors who passively went along and enforced the decrees? If they had stood up for what their professions demanded, if the doctors had cared about human life and the lawyers about justice, there would have been no need to ask years later "What happened to God?" Where was the voice of the church, so quick to protest when less is at stake than several million lives? Where were the Allied governments, who managed to look the other way and could find no room in their own countries for refugee Jews? We have a right to ask, "Where was God in 1940?" but we have a duty to ask "Where was Man? What could he have done to prevent the Holocaust?

In fact, where is Man most of the time? In what sort of activity does he spend most of his time, substance and energy? If we could take a candid snapshot of the human race at some random moment and tabulate what people were doing — their jobs, their leisure time activities — I suspect the results would not be flattering.

Author Wright Morris tried to do something like that in his novel *One Day.* I am sure that every one of you can remember exactly where you were and what you were doing on Friday afternoon, November 22, 1963 when you heard that President Kennedy had been killed. Morris, in his book, takes a group of typical people in a small town in California and shows where they were and what they were doing on that afternoon that was about to be burned unforgettably into their memory.

And what were they doing? Their activities ranged from the banal and trivial to the blatantly criminal. His point is that most of the time, the question "Where is Man?" will elicit a rather unflattering answer. Most of the time, the answer would be the same as it was in the Garden of Eden: with a whole wide world of sublime possibilities open to him, Man is hiding from himself, from God and from his responsibilities.

Today of course we know we are going to get our spiritual picture taken so we are on our good behavior. But what about the other days of the year, when the candid snapshot will show what we really look like? The great metaphor of Yom Kippur is the all-seeing eye and the book of deeds in which all of our actions are recorded. It is not just what we do today; it is what we do every day that defines us.

Today every seat in the synagogue is filled, but what about next week and the Shabbat after that? There will be empty seats in the synagogue and those empty seats will ask, "Where is man?" What happened to all those good intentions that were evident on Yom Kippur? Where is Man, what is he doing when he might be worshipping his Creator, when he might be learning to be grateful for the world he has been given?

There are books, rich in ideas, books that could enrich us, inspire us, enlarge our world, and they will be asking, "Where is Man?

Where is someone to take us down off the shelf, blow the dust off our ideas and give them life?"

There is a world full of possibilities; things crying to be done, human needs and spiritual opportunities, and that world will ask, "Where is Man?"

The question "Where is Man?" has special poignancy for many of us this Yom Kippur morning, because at the same time that we are so mindful of the full synagogue, we recall people who are not here today, the ones we will be thinking of at the Yizkor service. And as we remember them, we cannot help asking, "Where are they now, those people who were a part of our world?"

Well, where are they? If we are different people because the orbit of their lives intersected ours, because they taught us character and self-respect and pride in who we are, that is where we will find them today, in our character and our self-respect. If we find ourselves at services today because we remember them, because they schooled us in reverence, in cherishing memories, that is where they are today. If our experience of bereavement has made us more compassionate, more considerate of others, more patient with people, that is how the people we recall today take on reality and meaning.

Yom Kippur with its urgent message to us to transform ourselves is more than half over. With every passing hour, there is less reason to ask "Where is Man today?" and more reason to ask, "Where will he be tomorrow and next week and next month?" Will he have become the *briah hadasha*, the new person that Yom Kippur calls on him to be? Will he have come out of hiding, no longer afraid of facing God, no longer afraid of being human? Will he take on the responsibilities the world calls on him to assume?

There is a legend about one of the sages who was about to travel from the Land of Israel to Rome. The night before he left, he had a dream in which he saw a beggar dressed in rags sitting at the gate to Rome, and a voice in his dream said to him, "That is the Messiah, dressed as a beggar." The sage awoke and could not get that dream out of his mind as he made his way to Rome. As he approached the end of his journey, there was that man dressed in rags, exactly as he had seen him in his dream. The sage went up to him and said, "Is it true that you are the Messiah?" The man nodded. The sage asked "Then what are you doing here at the gate to Rome?" "Waiting." "Messiah, in a world so full of misery and hatred and war, a world in which the people of Israel is oppressed, a world where children go hungry and innocent people die, Messiah, in the name of God, what are you waiting for?" And the Messiah answered, "I was waiting for you, so that I could ask you, in the name of God, what are you waiting for?"

When we are tempted to ask. "Where is God in this cruel and chaotic world?" let us try to remember that God is where He has always been, waiting for us to fulfill our role in redeeming His world, and the real question is, as it has always been, "Where is Man?"

This sermon was delivered

six weeks after

my father's death at age 84.

How To Live Forever

Yom Kippur 1984

It is hard for me not to speak personally this morning. As most of you know, my father died six weeks ago. During the last weeks of his illness and in the time since his death, I found myself once again confronting the issue of mortality: how fragile a vessel the human body is, how weak and vulnerable. I found myself contemplating what our being alive consists of while we are alive, and what remains of all our doing, all our busyness and urgent activity after we have died.

There are prayers being uttered today that are not found in any prayerbook. There are times in the service, especially today on Yom Kippur, when we ignore the prayers printed in the Mahzor and offer instead the prayers issuing from our hearts, the fears, the apprehensions - who shall live and who shall die? For whom does the New Year hold a year of health in store, and for whom illness? What is going to happen to us for good or for ill in the coming months?

That sets up a kind of dialogue, a tension between us and the Mahzor, between the meditations of our hearts and the words of the printed page. The prayerbook says to us "Let's talk about how you haven't always been as good a person as you might have been last year." And we say, "No, that's not what I want to talk about. That's not my agenda. I want to talk about whether all the members of my family will still be here at this time next year. I want to talk about my fears about my job. I want to talk about whether my children and grandchildren will be continuations of who I am. I want to talk about the chest pains that wake me up in the middle of the night and the shortness of breath when I climb stairs."

And at that point, the prayerbook says to us "Come on, one day a year you get to talk to God, and all you can think of saying to Him is that you're tired and out of shape! You know, you're really not much of a conversationalist. I don't know why He puts up with you. But all right. You don't want to talk about sin; you don't want to talk about religion. You want to talk about life. Here, read these prayers. They'll teach you about life. They'll teach you that praying for life is more than just a matter of asking to still be here a year from now. It's a matter of what will you do with another year of life if you get it? It's not just, "What is your blood pressure?" "But, What are your values?"

It is a scene that has been played before many times over. One of the first, probably the most familiar, example of this dialogue occurs in the Bible, in the Book of Kings. King David has just died. Solomon his son has succeeded him, and one night, right after Solomon has taken on this massive responsibility, he has a dream in which God appears to him. God says, "As a final courtesy to your father David, and to help you be an effective monarch in his place, I am prepared to grant you one wish. Any one thing you want, you may have."

Solomon hears himself think aloud in his dream: My first instinct would be to pray for life and health. Ask the average person what one thing he wants more than anything, and it will be a long, healthy life. But I have seen animals live a long time, and I want more than that for my life. And I know than even the longest life ends sometime. I want my life to mean something.

"My next instinct would be to ask for success, to do all the things I want to do in life and to do them well. But I have seen people whose first wish was for success and too often, even if they get it (and generally people get what they want most in life and then are surprised when they get the bill for it), too often they end up lonely, disappointed people."

So Solomon turns to God and says, "If I can really have any one thing, what I want most is wisdom. I want, not a good heart that will beat regularly for ninety years and never give me pain, but a good heart that will know right from wrong, that will be able to tell the difference between a good person and an evil one, between an honest man and a liar. I want a heart that will cause me a great deal of pain as it contemplates all the anguish and the unfairness of life."

One suspects that Solomon must have been pretty wise to begin with, to know that wisdom is the most precious thing to ask for. But what is wisdom? What is it that he asked for, and God granted? Wisdom is more than just being smart, more than knowing a lot. Wisdom is first of all a sense of value, an ability to know the difference between the important and the trivial, between the enduring and the ephemeral. Oscar Wilde once defined a cynic as a man who knew the price of everything and the value of nothing. The flip side of that, I guess, would be to define a wise person as someone who measured something not by what it cost but by what it was truly worth. He would invest himself, not in a new car or fancy clothes, but in loyalty and friendship and being helpful to others, because they don't depreciate with time.

When you endure the loss of someone you love, the wisdom that comes with that experience comes in two parts. The first lesson is that no one lives forever. Good people, well-loved people — they die as inexorably as anyone else. When you have learned that, when you have accepted the inevitability of death, you're ready for the second lesson, which is, when a person dies, a very special part of him does not die but lives on. Bereavement is not just a lesson in losing; it is a lesson in keeping, an experience of immortality. Sometimes it takes death to make clear to us what the immortal part of a person is. Sometimes it is only when someone dies that you discover what part of him will live forever.

My father was a successful businessman, but what I will inherit from him will be less the fruits of that success, and more the sense of integrity he brought to his business dealings. He taught me long ago that you don't try to get away with something, even if you are sure that you won't be caught, because it's not right, and if it's not right, you will pay the price for it sooner or later in one way or another. And that is a part of him that did not die last August. When I was growing up, I had many occasions to clash with him because he could be a very controlling person, but I don't ever remember having to question his honesty or his moral integrity. When he became successful late in life, he would complain at length about the amount of taxes he had to pay, but it never occurred to him to cheat on his tax returns, to find ways to hide money. People would tell him, for example, that he could save on New York City and state taxes by establishing a paper residence in some other state, and buying but not using airline tickets to prove that he spent six months a year out of New York. But he couldn't play the game that way. No amount of money was worth the loss of his sense of moral integrity. When I was young and impressionable, the thing that mattered most conspicuously to my parents naturally became important to me. And that's where their immortality rests. That is the part of them that death could not put an end to.

How sad it is when somebody is given life and health, and doesn't do anything with it. If you have young children, when was the last time your children saw you get upset about something? Did they see you angry when the referee called a questionable penalty against the Patriots? Did they see you get angry when you got your bill from the Temple? Or did they see you get angry when there was a newscast about hunger and poverty somewhere in the world, or about political corruption and misuse of power, or when the U.N. mindlessly condemned Israel? What are you telling them is important, and what is trivial? What are you teaching your children to care about?

Because no matter how well you take care of yourself, no matter how much you exercise and watch your diet, your body won't last forever. It is vulnerable to so many kinds of illness and injury. But your anger, your laughter, your smile, your enthusiasm, your beliefs and your priorities, they're not subject to illness or decay. They will outlast you, so give thought to what kind of immortality you want.

To identify yourself as a Jew and then never do anything about it — not prayer and not study and not charity and not the books you read and not the meetings you go to — is to teach your family that being Jewish is an empty vessel, a label without content. And then we wonder why our children hold it cheap. Where do you suppose they learned that being Jewish need never inconvenience them in any significant way? Who taught them to perceive a Judaism without demands, without sacrifices, a Judaism that gives and never asks you to give anything back?

A colleague of mine recently wrote that for years he has been telling people that the home should support what is taught in the Religious School or Jewish education will be ineffective. And only now has he realized that he has been wrong all these years, he has had it backwards. It really works the other way around. The school's job is to deepen and reinforce what is taught at home, because the child spends so much more time at home and it's so much more important to him. No matter how good the school is, a child will live by what he is taught at home.

I didn't become a rabbi because I saw my father involved in synagogue work. If anything, it should have discouraged me to hear him come home and complain about what went on at board meetings. But I became a serious Jew because of his example. I learned something about values and priorities. If you can handle the idea that you're not going to live forever (that's the first step, and it's a big one), and if you can think of your children and grandchildren as your vicarious immortality, then don't pray for a year of life. Pray instead for the strength to do what you know you should be doing, but it's hard and it's unfamiliar. It means change, and change is always painful and frightening. But do you know what it feels like to have your children admire you because you stand for something? Is it worth a measure of discomfort and awkwardness to feel that?

Told he could ask for anything in the world and it would be granted, Solomon asked for wisdom, for a heart that would know right from wrong, and his wish was granted. How did this wisdom manifest itself? In the very next chapter, two women appear before Solomon with a newborn baby, each claiming to be the rightful mother. You know the story: Solomon orders the baby cut in half and each claimant given half. The true mother says "No, let her have the child, but let him live," and Solomon recognizes her as the true mother. How did he know to do that? Solomon had never been a mother, but he knew what a mother's heart would feel. There is no book you can read, no course you can take to teach you those things. That's wisdom, to be able to reach outside of yourself, and feel what is in another person's heart.

The person whose life is wrapped up in himself, who understands only what he is feeling - his life will end when he dies. But the person who has Solomon's heart of wisdom will find his way into the hearts of others and he will live on in them.

During the week that I was sitting shiva at the end of August, the story I found myself repeating most often about my father was about how one of his brothers stayed behind in Lithuania to take care of the elderly parents when the rest of the family emigrated. In1940, Stalin sent him to Siberia, to a town not far from the Arctic Circle, and for fifteen years, we never heard from him. We didn't know if he was alive or dead. Then, after Stalin died in 1953, there was a thaw in the Cold War and letters began to arrive from my uncle, first to relatives in Israel and then to us in America. My father sent him money to move back to Lithuania, to Vilna, and visited him there.

When Lithuanian Jews were permitted to leave to go to Israel, they were permitted to take only a few personal belongings and very little money. Some of them would sell all they had and give the money to my uncle. He would then write my father in code and my father would send the equivalent sum of money to the person when he arrived in Israel. These were not small sums. They added up to thousands of dollars a year. There was, of course, no publicity. There were no tax deductions to take. It was pure tzedakah. And in Vilna, and in Tel Aviv and in Petach Tikva, and in Los Angeles, there are people living better lives today because of that. My father never formed the habit of living to the limit of his income and then looking to see if there was anything left over for charity. He taught me something about how to live so that other people will live because of you. And today when I get letters telling me what my book or my lecture or my personal intervention has meant to someone, I know where I learned that lesson, and pray that my own daughter is learning it from me. That is the sort of wisdom that helps life transcend mere biological existence and makes your life matter.

My friends, we misunderstand this morning's service if we think that coming to shul and offering Yizkor prayers is an act of kindness for the deceased, something we do for them. It is in fact something we ask them to do for us, to teach us something about immortality. Our being here today testifies to the fact that they knew how to cheat death at least in part, how to live forever.

We may think our Yom Kippur prayers are for life, but on every page, the prayerbook tries to remind us: "It's not life; it's what you are going to do with your life. It's not length of days; it's breadth and depth of days. Not how many days there are, but how full they are and what they are filled with."

So don't just pray for a year of life and health. Pray as Solomon did, for the wisdom to make good use of the life and health you will be given, because even a long life won't last forever, but a good life connects to the essence of immortality and finds ways of continuing beyond itself. Since we can't pray to live forever, pray to stand for something, so that your life will be a story of values, and not just of duration. If the value of life is determined not by its length but by its content, by its meaning for others, if what we remember about people today is not how long they lived or how long ago they lived but what they taught us and how we are different because of them, then let us do as Solomon did, and look beyond the natural instinct to pray for length of days. Let us pray instead for wisdom, for the discerning heart that will know the difference between what is real and what is trivial. Let us pray for the courage to do things differently because the way we have been doing them just isn't good enough.

In the words of the psalmist, the ninetieth psalm: *Y'mey shnot-enu shivim shana*: The average person lives seventy years, some a little longer, some not nearly that long, and in either event, nobody lives as long as he would like to. *Limnot yameynu ken hoda v'navi l'vav hochmah*; so teach us to number our days so that we may get a heart of wisdom. Teach us that when we live wisely, when we care, when we share, when we stand for something besides our own well-being, our heart of wisdom never fails us and we do live forever.

I GAVE THIS SERMON on the Friday night of our son
Aaron's Bar Mitzvah Shabbat. Aaron suffered
from a rare and incurable disease. At age thirteen,
he was already very sick and frail, but bright and
courageous. He did wonderfully at the
Bar Mitzvah service but died less than a year
later. Decades after his death, his friends and
classmates continue to be inspired by his courage.
I think you will understand why I chose this story
as the basis for my sermon that Shabbat.

THE KERCHIEF

3 December 1976

The Israeli author, Shai Agnon, won the Nobel Prize for Literature in 1966 for, in the words of the Committee, "capturing the spirit of the Jewish people in his writings." He was born in Eastern Europe in a small town in Poland in 1888, and died in Jerusalem in 1970, four years after coming to international fame. Given when and where Agnon lived and died, it was perhaps inevitable that he would capture the spirit of the Jewish people, their transition from the Old World to the New, in his own biography and in his writings, and, more than any other modern author, would put the emphasis on what the Jewish people lost in the process.

I would speak tonight about one of my favorite Agnon stories, *Hamitpahat*, The Kerchief. In the story, the narrator looks backs upon his boyhood, his years of growing up. He remembers how his father would have to travel to the big city of Lashkovitz, to a fair, which all the merchants from the area had to attend. It was very dangerous and a very lonesome time for the boy and his mother to be left alone.

In the opening lines of the story, he describes the days when his father was away as days of mourning, like Tisha Ba'av, and the day he returned as being a Yom Tov, a festival. Meanwhile, the boy is going to school, and one of the things he is learning is the legend of the Messiah, how the Messiah sits every day in the gates of Rome, unrecognized and abused, disguised as a beggar. But one day he will stand up and reveal his true identity and redeem the world. He will remove all evil and suffering from it. And the boy, seeing the world through his own young eyes, dreams of this Messianic Age, a world without evil and without suffering. How does he picture it? He pictures it as a world in which his father will no longer have to go off to the fair, but will be able to stay home and be with him, and, together, they will stroll in the courtyards of a rebuilt temple in Jerusalem.

One day, his father comes back from the fair bringing presents for the family, and for the boy's mother he brings a beautiful kerchief. It's the eve of the Sabbath and she puts it on to light the candles. From that time on, she wears it only on Shabbat and Yom Tov. As the boy remembers it, the kerchief always remained immaculately clean. His mother never permitted a stain or a drop of dirt to come upon it. As the boy grows up and becomes Bar Mitzvah, his mother gives him the kerchief, puts it around his neck on the Sabbath of his Bar Mitzvah, and urges him to take care of it.

One day, shortly after that, a beggar comes to their town, an ugly, unkempt, disheveled-looking beggar. Everyone shuns him. Nobody gives him food. Nobody gives him money. They won't even let him into the synagogue to pray with them. The boy sees this beggar sitting forlorn on the steps of the synagogue where he was not permitted to enter. He goes over to the beggar, impulsively takes the kerchief from around his neck, and gives it to the beggar. The beggar uses it to wrap up the bleeding sores on his feet. When the boy realizes what he has done, he feels guilty. This, after all, was his mother's kerchief, which she always kept so immaculately clean, never permitted a spot of dirt to come upon, and here he has given it to this beggar to wrap his bleeding feet in. But he feels guilty only for a moment, for the sun comes out and shines on him and warms him, and that makes him feel better. He returns home, and his mother somehow knows what he has done. She is looking out through the window, smiling approvingly at him, and he feels reassured.

That's the story. What is it about? What is Agnon trying to tell us? As I understand it, it's a coming-of-age story. It's one of a genre of stories of a boy growing up and finding out about the real world, a story of how pain and suffering are permitted for the first time to intrude into the otherwise innocent, idyllic world of a child.

An interesting sidelight on the story: Agnon wrote it originally as a Bar Mitzvah present for 13-year-old Gershon Schocken, the son of his patron and publisher Zalman Schocken. Gershon's Bar Mitzvah was supposed to take place in Berlin in the spring of 1933. But (speak of a young man finding out about the real world), for reasons that I think you can understand, it took place a year later in Jerusalem. It is a story of a boy growing up, so that in the beginning of the story his only understanding of suffering, of problems, is his own loneliness, his own needs. But by the end of the story, he has learned that other people suffer more, and he has to take note of their needs as well.

It is sometimes called an "initiation story," and perhaps the prime example of it is the story of the Buddha, the founder of the Buddhist religion. He was born Prince Gautama, the young son of a wealthy, noble Indian family. His father wanted to make sure that his young son was protected from all knowledge of illness, death and ugliness. He built a high wall around the family estate and didn't permit anyone to enter, no servant, no family member, no delivery man, unless he was tall and handsome and physically fit, so that his young child growing up would never have to confront ugliness or sickness or deformity. One day, young Prince Gautama was playing ball (he must have been a young teenager) on the lawn of his estate. The ball bounced over a fence, and he climbed over the fence to try to find it. There, on the other side, he found sick and old and crippled and maimed and deformed and dying people, people the likes of whom he had never seen before in his life. According to the Buddhist legend, he was so overcome by this, he sat down under a tree (which was soon to become one of the holy places in Buddhism) and said, "I won't move from here until I have understood how such things can exist in God's beautiful world."

This is the crisis that a young child growing up has to go through. In the Agnon story, the kerchief functions as a religious symbol. It's a kind of a tallit. It is put on the boy's shoulders by his parents when he becomes a Bar Mitzvah. It is used only on the Sabbath and Yom Tov. Frequently, Agnon uses the symbol of the tallit to talk about that which links God to the Jewish people, which, of course, is authentically one of the things that a tallit is about.

One of the most beautiful and one of the most famous lines in all of Agnon's stories is the opening line of *Agunot;* "It is taught: a thread of grace is spun and drawn out of the deeds of Israel, and the Holy One, blessed be He, Himself sits and weaves strand by strand, a tallit all grace and all mercy for the Congregation of Israel to deck herself in." And when Agnon describes the boy giving the tallit to the beggar, I think one of the things he is saying is that the purpose of religion is to reach out and help people, to assuage their pain, and not only to turn in on yourself and make yourself feel good. Childish religion guides a person to deal only with his own needs, his own problems, what makes him feel better. More mature religion sees God as moving you to reach out and help somebody else. For this tallit, for this immaculately clean kerchief to be soiled because it's given to the beggar, for Agnon, is not a sin or a sacrilege, it is the highest order of religious action. It is something of which both God and other people approve, as symbolized by the sun shining on the boy and warming him, and by his mother's smile of approval. There is something lacking in a religion that refuses to involve itself in the messiness of the world.

Why does the boy give the kerchief to the beggar? Did you understand that in the story? He does it because he wants to bring the Messiah, because he remembers all those legends of how the Messiah comes somewhere disguised as a beggar, and because nobody recognizes him and responds to him and nobody is kind to him, he goes away without revealing his identity and without redeeming the world. The boy wants to bring the Messiah so his father won't have to travel to Lashkovitz anymore, but can stay home with him. And in doing this, he learns a very important lesson: *you can bring the Messiah for somebody else much more easily than you can for yourself.* He doesn't bring his own redemption; he brings the beggar's redemption.

This, I think, is what it means to be grown up. It means finally coming to terms with the world's imperfections, realizing that the world is a much more complicated place than you used to think, and putting your own problems in the context of the whole world's rough edges and unevenness. The child thinks that he can bring the Messiah and make the whole world perfect. The adult understands how much he can do to bring the Messiah for other people, and hopes that somewhere there will be someone to bring the Messiah for him. He understands how much he can do to alleviate other people's problems more readily than his own, and if that doesn't make the whole world perfect, at least it makes his corner of the world discernibly better. And as the boy finds out at the end of the story, that can be a very exalting and a very satisfying feeling.

That is why Agnon wanted to tell this story to 13-year old Gershon Schocken, and why I wanted to share it with you tonight.

Our son Aaron died in November 1977.

Yom Kippur the following fall

was a step in my transition from

the year of mourning to the permanence

of life without him. This was my

sermon that Yom Kippur morning.

The Missing Piece (1978)

In memory of Aaron Zev Kushner 1963-1977
Yom Kippur

Though we are all here in the same place at the same time for Yom Kippur, each of us comes with his own very personal agenda, his own hopes, dreams, fears, hurts, memories. I suspect that is always the case when a large number of people congregate, but especially today, when the setting calls forth so many deeply personal responses. The prayerbook tries to pull us together by asking us to share the same words, but it's not really enough.

The prayerbook tries to get us talking about sin and repentance, about cleansing and atonement. But our hearts resist. We don't respond to sin, to atonement. We need to pray about the brevity of life, the pain of death and loss, the sustaining power of memory. And so strong are we in our insistence, in the gravitational pull we exercise on the service, that the service finally has to accommodate us. When we open the Torah on Yom Kippur to study the ancient rituals of purification, the opening words deal not with Yom Kippur but with life and death:

"The Lord spoke to Moses after the death of the two sons of Aaron the High Priest," as if the Torah itself had to concede that it can't begin to talk of atonement and cleansing until it has spoken of grief and bereavement first, because that is where our hearts are.

Let me begin by telling you a story, a strange kind of story, which can best be described as a children's story for grownups. It was written by a man named Shel Silverstein, and it's called "The Missing Piece."

Once upon a time, there was a circle that was missing a piece and it was very unhappy. It went all over the world looking for its missing piece, — over hills and across rivers, up mountains and down into valleys, through rain and snow and blistering sun, it went looking for its missing piece. And wherever it went, because it was missing a piece, it had to go very slowly. So as it went along, it stopped to look at the flowers and talk to the butterflies. It stopped to rest in the cool grass. Sometimes it passed a snail, and sometimes the snail passed it. And wherever it went, it kept looking for its missing piece.

But it couldn't find it. Some pieces were too big and some were too small; some were too square and some were too pointy. None of them fit. Then suddenly one day, it found a piece that seemed to fit perfectly. The circle was whole again; nothing was missing. It took the piece into itself and started to roll away. And now, because it was a whole unbroken circle, it could roll much faster. And so it rolled quickly through the world, past the lakes and past the forests, too fast to get a good look at them. It rolled too quickly to notice the flowers, too fast for any of the insects to fly by and talk to it. And when the circle realized that it was rolling too fast to do any of the things it had been doing for years, it stopped, it very reluctantly put down its missing piece, and it rolled slowly away, heading out into the world, looking for its missing piece.

Now that is such a beautiful story, I almost don't want to spoil it, to violate its poignancy, by taking it apart and trying to understand it. But it is saying some important things. And the most important thing it is saying is that, in a strange, mysterious way, which we can't really understand, a person is more whole when he is incomplete, when he is missing something. That little bit of incompleteness cures him of his illusion of self-sufficiency, opens him up — as it did to the circle in the story — to feeling more, seeing more, experiencing more. In a paradoxical way, the man who has everything will never have some of the most poignantly beautiful experiences in life. The man who has everything will never know what it feels like to yearn, to hope. He will never understand the songs and poetry that are born out of longing, out of grieving, out of incompleteness. You can never make him happy by giving him something he would enjoy, because by definition, he already has it. In a strange way, the person who has everything, who is missing absolutely nothing, is a very poor person indeed.

We are more complete if we are incomplete. That is the paradoxical truth of the story. We are made more whole by the things we don't have. I think that's true at many levels. When it comes to giving charity, we become more whole through what we give away. I think we instinctively understand that the person who can afford to be generous, who can afford it psychologically and not only financially, is a more whole person than the man who is afraid to part with what he has because he's afraid that if he gives something away, he's giving away part of himself. The wealthy man who needs to be asked three times before he gives, and thanked three times afterwards, strikes us as, in some ways, an incomplete person. He may have a lot of money but he's lacking something more important. The man who is not afraid to be generous, because he knows he is not giving his self away, comes across as really more whole.

It is perhaps indicative of the culture we live in that many of us are familiar with the parable of the Fish and the Loaves from the New Testament — how a whole crowd of people were miraculously fed with just two fishes and seven loaves of bread, — but we don't know that the story originally comes from the Hebrew Bible, where it's told about the prophet Elisha:

A man came to Elisha with a present of a loaf of bread and an ear of corn. And the prophet told him, "Distribute it to the entire crowd!" The man said, "What! Am I supposed to divide this among a hundred people?" And the prophet told him, "Distribute it to all the people for the Lord has said, it will suffice." And he gave it to them, and they ate, and left some over, as the Lord had promised. (2 Kings 4:42-44).

It's a nice trick to know when you have unexpected company. But the real point of the story is a more profound one. Each of us has the resources — the financial and emotional resources — to help a whole lot of people, but we don't know how much we have until we start giving them away. It's a scary thing, I can tell you from my experience as a Rabbi, to have people make emotional demands on you, to have them ask you to give them strength. That's why it's so much easier to find people to work with machines, with numbers, with pieces of paper, and so much harder to find people who can work with people. You're afraid that if you give them strength, you'll be left weak. But in fact, it works just the other way. The act of strengthening others makes you even stronger. The process of giving away leaves you more complete for having done it, like the pitcher of wine in Greek mythology that grew magically more and more full as people tried to empty it. You never know how rich and full you are till you start sharing yourself with others.

The person who has grown comfortable with the fact that he's missing a piece is, in a sense, more whole than the person who thinks he has to be complete, unbroken. When someone you love has died, there is no replacing that person. His or her death leaves an emptiness that will never be filled. A husband or wife can remarry and be very happy, a son can invest more of himself in his own family, a grieving parent in her remaining children. But whatever you do, you will go through life with a piece of you missing. No matter how full, no matter how crowded your life may go on to become, there will always be that empty space.

But the person who has survived bereavement (and that's all you can ever do with it, — survive; you can't prevent it or undo it or ignore it) the person who has survived and learned that losing part of yourself is an inevitable part of life, has become a more complete person than he could ever have been before. Nothing can scare you because you have been through the worst, and come through it.

The person I feel closest to in all the pages of the Bible is a man whose name I don't even know. All I know about him is one poem he wrote 2700 years ago, the 30th Psalm. We recite this psalm every morning at the beginning of the service and after we've said it, if there is a minyan present, the mourners say Kaddish.

The 30th Psalm is the story of a man who used to believe that nothing bad could ever happen to him. "I once thought, while at ease, nothing could shake my security." And he was profoundly and sincerely grateful to God for being so good to him. In exchange, the man lived a moral life, prayed regularly, and gave charity. Then suddenly, a series of terrible calamities befell him. "You turned Your face from me, and I was terrified." His whole world threatened to fall apart.

But then he made a vital discovery. He learned something about himself he could never have known before, — that he was capable of believing in God and in God's world even when tragedy happened to him instead of to strangers. Before that, he could never have been sure of the quality of his faith. Did he serve God because He was God, or because God was good to him? Now he knows what he could only have hoped before, that there is nothing tentative, nothing conditional or self-centered about his faith. In a sense, God has given him something he had never had before, the strength to go on despite his wounds, despite his sorrow. That's a great thing for God to give him; how could he have found his way without it?

In that same mysterious way of which we have spoken, there is something whole about his faith now, where it was immature and incomplete before. Missing a piece has somehow made him whole. The religion of "I love You, God, as long as You're good to me" has been replaced by, "I love You because You're God and because without You, I couldn't have made it."

It's not only bereavement that forces us to go through that process. Every one of us has come here as an incomplete, unfulfilled person in one way or another. Some of us have been left incomplete by death, some by a divorce — a part of ourselves has moved out of our lives and somewhere out there, somebody is walking around with some of our most intimate memories, – others of us by disappointment, the job we wanted and didn't get, the talent that would have made us so happy, that we somehow never managed to develop, the child who didn't turn out as we hoped he would. Every one of us is incomplete in one way or another. We're missing something from our lives, and its absence weighs us down, slows us down (like the circle in the story), compels us to see everything in our lives a little bit differently.

Yet I would insist that we're made more whole by the experience of missing something. We learn reality, we come to see the world as it really is. The world isn't a birthday party, where if you've been good, everything happens the way you want it to. It's a very mixed-up unpredictable place, where hours of sunshine alternate with hours of darkness, redeemed by occasional flashes of bravery and love.

We learn gratitude. Precisely because we can't have everything, we learn to be grateful for what we do have. Children don't understand that. For them, the world is divided into what they have, and what they don't have yet, but intend to have. It is hard for them to understand the idea that there are some things they won't ever have, and that some of the things they have may be taken away from them. And probably that's just as well. They deserve a few years to be children; they'll be wise long enough. But we who roll through life slowly, with our missing pieces — we understand that.

In the Grace after Meals (and you'll have to forgive me on this of all days for speaking earlier of feeding the multitude, and now of the Birkat Mazon, the Grace after Meals), there is a line toward the end: "May God bless me and those around me as He blessed

Abraham, Isaac and Jacob, *biv'racha shlemah*, with a complete blessing, with everything, a blessing from which nothing is lacking." And the Midrash, the commentary, notes, "Maybe Abraham, Isaac, and Jacob were blessed by God with a blessing from which nothing was missing. But nobody since then has been."

And in fact, when you think about it, Abraham, Isaac, and Jacob had their missing pieces as well. They all had problems with their parents, their wives, their children. Abraham broke with his father over a matter of religion, left him and never saw him again. He sent one of his wives out of his house into the desert. He had a son who intermarried and caused him grief.

Isaac was almost killed by his father as a child. When he grew old, he lived with his wife and children but had nothing to say to them. They were living in opposite directions, they had forgotten how to trust each other.

Jacob ran away from home as a teenager. He quarreled with his father, with his brother, with his father-in-law, and he saw his sons quarrel bitterly with each other. How can they be described in the Bible as receiving a complete blessing with nothing missing?

The fact of the matter is, there is no such thing as a life that isn't missing a piece. It can't be a full life without disappointment, without pain, without loss. Maybe that's what the prayer really means when it says that Abraham, Isaac and Jacob received a complete blessing. Maybe it doesn't mean that they got everything they wanted and kept it. Maybe it means that God gave them a full life, a life full of love and full of pain (because how can there be love without pain?), a life full of hope and full of disappointments (because if you hope grandly enough, you'll have your share of disappointments). Maybe instead of giving them an easy life, God gave them a full life, the blessing of fullness, a life full of joy and full of tears, full of accomplishment and full of failure. And we ask that God give us that kind of fullness, that kind of wholeness, too.

To be missing a piece, to have to go through life carrying around an emptiness where something important and precious to you used to be, and to understand that despite the pain you are a deeper and richer person because you're missing that piece — that's what it means to be whole. That Hassidic master, the Kotzker Rebbe, used to say, "There is nothing in all the world as whole as a broken heart," and sooner or later in this life, each of us comes to understand what he meant.

The Torah makes the same point. In the opening lines of the Book of Leviticus, when it speaks of how our forefathers used to worship God with animal offerings, it says *"adam ki yakriv, When a man brings a sacrifice."* Several times, for each of the categories of offering, it repeats those words, *"adam ki yakriv,* when a man brings a sacrifice." Then, when it comes to the very last kind of offering, the mincha, the poor man's offering, it suddenly changes the wording, and now it says *"nefesh ki takriv,* When a soul brings a sacrifice."

The commentators respond to the change of language and ask, what kind of sacrifice does a soul bring? This is their answer: Sometimes there is something you want very badly, to the very depths of your soul. You work for it, you pray for it, you say to yourself and to God that if you could only have that, you'd be happy, you wouldn't want anything else. But one day you have to acknowledge that it's not going to happen, like Moses at the end of the Torah, realizing that he's never going to reach the goal he has spent his life working for. If you can do that without losing your soul, without becoming so embittered that life will have no further meaning for you, if you can be like the circle at the end of the story, if you can let go of your missing piece and roll away to face life without it, that is *nefesh ki takriv,* that is the sacrifice of one's soul which we bring and lay on God's altar, and turn away, feeling whole in a way that we could never feel whole before.

*This was my sermon on the Friday night of
our daughter Ariel's Bat Mitzvah Shabbat.
To understand the opening lines of the sermon,
you need to know that our daughter is blessed with
a lovely singing voice, unlike either her father or
mother. She chanted the Kiddush prayer and sang
several selections with the Temple choir. She would
go on to study voice at New York University.*

THE STORY OF THE KIDDUSH CUP is completely
true. My father brought it up from New York
and gave it to Ariel for her Bat Mitzvah.
She uses it to this day. It may be the best sermon
I ever gave; it remains my personal favorite.

THE KIDDUSH CUP FROM MARIAMPOL (1979)

I trust you realize that what you have just experienced is a refutation of all modern theories of genetics. We still don't know from which remote ancestor, on either her father's or her mother's side, Ariel inherited her singing voice.

But as intriguing as the search for her musical forebear is the story of the silver cup over which she recited Kiddush. It came into the possession of our family just recently, but has quite a history behind it. Forty years ago, it was the Kiddush cup in the synagogue in Mariampol, the town in southern Lithuania from which my parents came. In 1940, when the Nazis invaded Lithuania, a woman who worked for the synagogue took it, with some of the other valuable ritual objects, and buried them to keep them from falling into Nazi hands. When the war ended and she had survived it, she went back and dug them up again. But now there were very few Jews left in Mariampol, and with Lithuania having come under Communist domination, prospects for the survival of Jewish life there were slim. When in 1950, one of the remaining Jews, a cousin of ours, left to go to Israel, the Kiddush cup was entrusted to him. He is an old man now, with no family, and so last spring he gave it to my father, so that it might continue to be used for sanctifying the Sabbath as it was in Mariampol. And my father brought it up from New York so that Ariel might say Kiddush over it tonight.

I was very moved when I heard that story of the Kiddush cup

that had been buried and dug up again, that had been hidden and reclaimed years later, because what is a Kiddush cup? It is a *kli kodesh*, a vessel of holiness, a symbol of our believing and proclaiming our belief. It is a vessel of remembering. In the prayer over it, we refer to *zikkaron l'maaseh breshit*, remembering God's creation of the world and seeing the world differently because this is a world God made. We refer to *zecher litziyat mitzrayim*, remembering how God freed us from Egyptian slavery. And it is a symbol of joy and celebration. It is the cup of wine with which we mark all the happy events in our lives.

And it occurred to me that it *is* the fate of a Kiddush cup to disappear and then to re-emerge, to be buried and go into hiding, and then to be reclaimed when years have passed and the war is over, because the things for which it stands – belief and memory and joy – that's what they do. They disappear and we think they are gone forever. But then one day they come back again. They go underground, and years later we find our way back to reassert our claim to them.

Some people can lift the Kiddush cup every day of their lives, week after week, their faith, their happiness remaining constant, even as some people can be married for forty years with never an angry word or disagreement. But for most of us, there is a tide to our religious feelings. There is an ebb and flow to our ability to believe, to celebrate. Faith and happiness are not constant. To paraphrase Ecclesiates, there is a time to bury the Kiddush cup and there is a time to reclaim it.

Some years ago, Gail Sheehy wrote a best-selling book called *Passages*. As some of you know, I didn't particularly like the book. I thought it was a manifesto for selfishness and loneliness. But the best part of the book, for me, was the sub-title "The Predictable Crises of Adult Life." I think that is an important idea, that some of the crises of our lives are predictable. Everybody goes through them, and we can know in advance that they are going to happen and that they will follow a certain course.

Things happen to us, almost predictably, which make us cast aside the Kiddush cup because we can't lift it and bless it without feeling like total hypocrites. Things happen which make it very hard for us to believe that this is God's world. The cup that Ariel said Kiddush over was buried forty years ago because the Nazis invaded Lithuania, and began rounding up and deporting Jews, because millions of innocent people were being killed for no reason. I suspect a lot of Kiddush cups were buried in those years, figuratively if not literally, by people who could not bring themselves to sing God's praises in a world where such things could happen.

That is virtually a predictable crisis of growing up, that at some point, you will have to confront the reality of evil. You will find yourself confronted by the unfairness of life. You will conclude that there is no God and all religion is just wishful thinking. We read of wars and accidents, we know instances of the wrong person getting sick and the wrong person losing his job, and it just doesn't make sense. We conclude, some in sadness and some in triumph, that this can't possibly be God's world, and we rule out of our lives for good the simple faith, the unquestioning acceptance of religion that we had when we were children. That is a predictable crisis of the spiritual life. It happens to almost all of us, and the more sensitive you are, that more you care about justice and fairness, the more sharply it hits you.

But the 15-year-old who tells me that he has become an atheist hasn't made his final judgment on the subject. Like the Kiddush cup that was buried during the years of the Holocaust and recovered afterwards, there comes a time when the ability to believe and the ability to bless come back to you. It doesn't happen because the world has changed or grown any less unfair; it happens because you have learned to see the world differently. The God you once believed in was a God of happy endings to every story, a God who would make everything smooth and painless. And you were right when you decided that such a God didn't exist. But then you came to know a God who could help people live meaningfully even without the happy endings, a God who taught wisdom and fortitude, so that people could find beauty and courage in the stories of their lives, no matter how they ended. There is a time to bury the Kiddush cup and a time to reclaim it, a time to lose faith in the world because it's not perfect and we want it to be perfect, and a time to recover our ability to believe in an imperfect world because we see people living in it with love and courage.

The predictable crises of growing up: one of them is the loss of memory. Not the kind of memory loss that affects old people, where they can remember word for word a conversation they had in 1926, but they can't remember that they already told you that story yesterday. I have in mind the memory loss that affects young people when they go off to college, and it's hard for them to remember that they are their parents' children. The Bibles, the Kiddush cups and candlesticks we gave them when they became Bar Mitzvah are left behind, with the other artifacts of adolescence, the reminders of the years when they had to do what their parents told them to. And along with that, they leave behind the Jewishness of their home, the moral stance of their parents and their community, as they exchange the parochialism of a suburban Jewish home for the equally narrow parochialism of the college campus. Those years are years of forgetting, forgetting who your parents and grandparents are and who they raised you to be.

Maybe they have to be, for that young person to achieve a measure of independence, to find out who he is and not only who others want him to be. If the forgetting were permanent, the Jewish community would be a terminal case. There would be no need for Rabbis, Cantors, or Hebrew School teachers beyond the end of the century. But one doesn't forget forever. Memories of Jewishness go underground. They maintain a subterranean existence through all those years, until one day, like the Kiddush cup from Mariampol, it's time for them to resurface. And then, one day when the whole wide world is too vast for the college graduate to live in and he wants the intimacy of his own home, his own family, he will go back and remember who he is, and remember what a home can be like. When he has fears and needs and questions that book learning can't help him with, when the medical student and the accountant and the business administration major realize that there has to be more to life that living as a doctor, or an accountant, or running a business, then they will remember and find their way back. And the Kiddush cup which had once been left behind with the toys of childhood will find its way back into their hands and onto their tables once more.

If you live long enough, if you care deeply enough, there will come a time when you will face another predictable crisis of adult spiritual life. You'll get hurt. Something will come along and take away the things, the people that make your life worthwhile, and you'll wonder if you'll ever be able to be happy again. If the Kiddush cup is the symbol of joy and celebration, you'll put it away, bury it in a drawer somewhere, because you will have no use for it. "Where is there joy?" you will ask, "Where is there anything to celebrate?" In the words of Kahlil Gibran, you will turn your back on the sun, and the sun will become for you nothing more than a caster of shadows.

And that's where the Kiddush cup will work its greatest miracle. It will find its way back from where you buried it, and force you to include it in your life. Miraculously, inexorably, the goodness of life will reassert itself. And the man who said he would never laugh again, will laugh; and the woman who insisted she had nothing left to live for, will find new reasons to get up in the morning and look forward to the day; and the house which had grown dark and still will echo once more with the sounds of celebration.

Our family, in looking forward to this very important and very fulfilling Shabbat, came gradually to focus on one verse from the Haftarah which Ariel will chant tomorrow morning. It seemed to summarize a lot of things for us: "Youths may grow faint and weary, young men may stumble and fail, but those who look to the Lord will have their own strength renewed. They shall run and not grow weary; they shall march and not grow faint." (Isaiah 40:31)

I think that is what God and religion and growing up are all about, that you don't have to despair when you go through the predictable crises of life, because they are not forever, and God gives a renewal of hope and strength to those who turn to Him. That's what God is, more than anything else. He is not just the Creator of the world; He is not just a father figure in Heaven, a parent who protects or a parent who punishes. God is the answer to the question of where people get the strength to go on when they have used up all of their strength, where people get hope when there seems to be no grounds for hope, where people get the capacity to go on enduring after they have reached the limits of their endurance. It happens all the time; I've seen it, we have all seen it. Those who are at the point of running out of strength, look to the Lord and their strength is renewed.

So that all who are starved for holiness, because they just can't believe this is God's world, may find a renewed belief; so that those who are confused and spiritually homeless because they have forgotten who they are and where they come from, may be helped to remember who they are and where they come from; so that those whom the pain of life has made strangers to joy and celebration may be given cause to rejoice once more, — we take the cup from where it was discarded, buried, and left behind, — we fill it with the symbols of the goodness and bounty of this world, and we lift it one more time in song and praise, in joy and in holiness, in memory and in celebration...L'hayyim, to life.